devotion
eXplOsiOn

devotion
eXplOsiOn

Getting Real with God

C h r i s t y   B o w e r

Discovery House Publishers

Books, music, and videos that feed the soul with the Word of God

Box 3566 Grand Rapids, MI 49501

Discovery House Publishers is affiliated with RBC Ministries, Grand Rapids, Michigan.

Discovery House books are distributed to the trade exclusively by Barbour Publishing, Inc., Uhrichsville, Ohio.

Requests for permission to quote from this book should be directed to: Permissions Department, Discovery House Publishers, P.O. Box 3566, Grand Rapids, MI 49501.

Scripture taken from the *New American Standard Bible,* © Copyright 1960, 1962, 1963, 1968, 1971, 1972, 1973, 1975, 1977, 1995 by the Lockman Foundation. Used by permission.

Library of Congress Cataloging-in-Publication Data
Bower, Christy, 1968–
    Devotion explosion : getting real with God / Christy Bower.
      p. cm.
    ISBN-13: 978-1-57293-229-6
    1. Spiritual life—Christianity. 2. Spirituality. I. Title.
BV4501.3.B69 2007
242—dc22

                        2007024378

Design and typesetting by Lakeside Design Plus

Printed in the United States of America

07 08 09 10 11 / SB / 10 9 8 7 6 5 4 3 2 1

Contents

Chapter One
An Appointment with Disappointment   7

Chapter Two
A Man's Best Friend   27

Chapter Three
Supplicate or Suffocate   46

Chapter Four
God's Word to Me   66

Chapter Five
Can You Hear Me Now?   85

Chapter Six
The Ultimate Reality Show   102

Chapter Seven
A List of Demands, or a Life of Devotion?   121

Chapter Eight
A Devotion Explosion   140

An Appointment with Disappointment

When I was a new believer, other more experienced believers instructed me to set aside a daily quiet time for Bible reading and prayer, with the general expectation that this should happen early every morning. The tools for this common practice included a Bible reading plan that I could check off each day and a journal or list of prayer requests that would enable me to gauge how effective my prayers were. Different believers taught me various formulas for how to pray.

One of the most popular formulas was the ACTS plan: Adoration, Confession, Thanksgiving, and Supplication. I could spend five minutes on each of these subject matters during prayer and mechanically work my way through a semi-robotic monologue with God, watching the clock the whole time. Then, if I spent another ten minutes reading the Bible, I would have completed a thirty-minute quiet time—the gold-star standard many believers strive for yet few successfully achieve on a consistent basis.

Although these methods were universally taught as standards for appropriate Christian discipline, everyone I knew confessed struggling to maintain a quiet time. The only thing more universal than the belief in these standards was the sense of failure and guilt people felt for not living up to them.

Perhaps you can identify with these frustrations. If you can, you're not alone. As king of Israel, Saul performed the required rituals that he assumed would please God. He sought the Lord's favor using the formulas that were prevalent in his day, but throughout the Old Testament Scriptures, we find that the Lord did not answer him. Saul's interactions with God were consistently an appointment with disappointment.

> If your time with God seems like an appointment with disappointment, get ready to have a devotion explosion as you learn new ways of having a more intimate, more satisfying, relationship with Him.

Let's begin by catching a glimpse of Saul's interactions with God, and then we will see what we can learn from his experience that will transform our own interactions with God. If your time with God seems like an appointment with disappointment, get ready to have a devotion explosion as you learn new ways of having a more intimate, more satisfying, relationship with Him.

Saul: "The Lord Did Not Answer Him"

The oil felt cool on Saul's sun-baked scalp. As the prophet Samuel poured the entire flask of oil over Saul's head, it ran down the young king's wavy locks of hair, even dripping off his beard. "The Lord has anointed you as leader over His inheritance," said Samuel.

After the two men discussed their plans to meet at Gilgal, they went their separate ways. Saul would arrive in Gilgal before Samuel. Samuel knew this, and he told Saul to wait for seven days, and then he would come and show Saul what to do. Along the way, Saul met some prophets on the road, and the Spirit of God came upon him so mightily that he prophesied with them.

Saul gathered an army of three thousand men. He commanded two thousand, while his son, Jonathan, was commander of a thousand. They all assembled at Gilgal for a great celebration with Saul, but the Philistines saw the gathering as an opportunity to attack, so they assembled nearby with soldiers as numerous as the sand. The small Israeli army began to scatter away to safety, hiding in caves. When Samuel did not arrive in seven days, Saul took matters into his own hands and offered up the burnt offering. Just then, Samuel arrived. "What have you done?" asked Samuel.

"You were late," scolded Saul, "and the Philistines were gathered in such number that my men began to flee, so I forced myself to offer the burnt offering to seek the Lord's favor."

Samuel shook his head. "You have not kept the command the Lord gave you, so as a consequence, your kingdom will not endure. God has appointed a new leader of His people."

After Samuel left, Saul counted six hundred men who remained with him, and none except Saul and Jonathan had sword or spear.

Suddenly, the ground shook, and God sent panic among the Philistine camp. Saul and his men went down to find the Philistines in such a state of confusion that they were killing each other. Seeing their opportunity, the Israelites who had hidden among the rocks came out to join the battle.

When evening came, Saul wanted to continue attacking the Philistines until dawn, but the priest wanted to inquire of God first. So Saul asked God, "Shall we attack the Philistines, and, if so, will You give us victory?" But God did not answer him.

Saul stopped pursuing the Philistines, but shortly thereafter Samuel sent word from the Lord that Saul should destroy the Amalekites and everything that belonged to them. So Saul and his army attacked them, taking King Agag hostage and keeping the best of the spoils.

> Does the Lord delight in burnt offerings, or in obedience? To obey is better than sacrifice.

After the battle, Samuel approached Saul saying, "Why do I hear the bleating of sheep and the lowing of cattle?"

Saul answered, "We spared the best of the sheep and cattle to sacrifice to the Lord."

"Stop!" yelled Samuel, his face flushed with anger. "Does the Lord delight in burnt offerings, or in obedience? To obey is better than sacrifice. You have rejected God's word; therefore, God has rejected you as king."

Saul begged for forgiveness, but after that the Spirit of the Lord departed from Saul and an evil spirit terrorized him.

For years, Saul lived in fear. When Saul faced the Philistine army once again, terror filled his heart. He inquired of the Lord, but the Lord did not answer him by prophets, in dreams, or by casting lots with the Urim.[1] In desperation, Saul sought

1. The Urim and Thummim were originally tools of the high priest, which were kept on his person in a breastplate of judgment (Exodus 28:30). No one knows what they looked like or exactly how they worked, but they were used to obtain answers from God. Like rolling dice or drawing lots from a container, the random results were believed to be controlled by God. However, something about the Urim and Thum-

out a medium in Endor, whom he persuaded to conjure up the spirit of the now-deceased Samuel. Saul pled with Samuel, "The Philistines are fighting against me and God no longer answers me, so I have called on you to tell me what to do."

"The Lord has become your enemy," said Samuel, "and tomorrow you and your sons will be with me."

Who's in Charge Here?

Saul demonstrated an independent spirit that wanted God to bless his decisions (1 Samuel 13:12). When it came right down to it, Saul would disobey God whenever it suited his purposes, as he did when he offered the sacrifice before Samuel arrived or when he kept the best of the Amalekites' livestock.

"God is my co-pilot" used to be a popular slogan. Christians feel pleased with themselves for inviting God along for the ride, but who's in charge if God is the co-pilot? Self. *I am in the pilot's seat. I am in control. I am the one barking orders to my co-pilot, who really doesn't know as much as I do about flying through life. Nonetheless, I'll bring along a co-pilot just in case I get in trouble and need some help.*

This misses the whole point of salvation. Your plane is spiraling out of control, headed for certain death and destruction, until you hand over the controls to God. He is the pilot now. He rights the ship and navigates a course for heaven that takes you through a very exciting journey along the way. With God in complete control, *you* are now the co-pilot, taking orders from God about how to navigate through the turbulent

---

mim allowed for a non-answer, as in the case of Saul, who was not able to receive answers from God in this manner (1 Samuel 28:6). Perhaps if the two objects came out with different answers, it was deemed as silence from God on the matter.

areas. (You don't get to be a backseat driver, either, barking orders to the pilot.)

This fundamental change of control needs to transform our perspective before we can experience the joys of a whole new level of communication in our relationship. Many believers still want to control everything, including their relationship with God. They need something they can control and quantify in order to measure their perceived spiritual growth, so they dedicate themselves to a quiet time schedule. Then they experience the ups and downs of trying to be successful at it.

Robert Mulholland describes spirituality as a journey, but he points out that most people view spirituality as a possession to be achieved: "Thus the endless quest for techniques, methods, programs by which we hope to 'achieve' spiritual fulfillment. The hidden premise behind all of this is the unquestioned assumption that we alone are in control of our spirituality."[2]

Saul was frustrated that God did not answer him, because God's response was the one element that Saul could not control. Saul performed the required rituals that he assumed would please God. Yet he did all these religious activities as a means to get what he wanted, as a means to manipulate God.

This manipulative control is pervasive in our thinking. Yet, disguised in a spiritual cloak, it can be difficult to identify. For instance, I often hear people say, "I give God 10 percent of my income so that the other 90 percent will go farther." Does that strike you as manipulative control of God for self-serving purposes? That's not giving; that's simply a business transaction or investment strategy. The Bible says we are to give expecting nothing in return (Luke 6:35). Yet our subtle manipulative ways

2. M. Robert Mulholland, Jr., *Invitation to a Journey: A Road Map for Spiritual Formation* (Downers Grove, Ill.: InterVarsity Press, 1993), 12.

clothe our true motives in spiritual sounding terms. Saul used this manipulative strategy when he disobeyed God's instruction to destroy the Amalekites and everything that belonged to them. He kept the best livestock and justified his actions to Samuel, saying, "The people took some of the spoil . . . to sacrifice to the LORD your God at Gilgal" (1 Samuel 15:21). Saul was trying to manipulate the situation to get what he wanted and cloaking it in terms that sounded spiritual.

Saul was obedient to a system; he was not obedient to God. When his army was fleeing from the Philistines at Gilgal, Saul took charge of the situation, racing ahead of God's plan and offering the sacrifice before the appointed time. His excuse for this act of disobedience was that he wanted God to bless his decision to proceed into battle. Essentially, in Saul's thinking, God was the co-pilot. Saul was in control, but he periodically sought the approval of his co-pilot. Although Saul was filled with the Spirit, he never gave God control of his life. His communication reflected that attitude, as he approached God with self-serving formality.

> When we give God control over our lives, it changes the way we communicate with Him.

When we give God control over our lives, it changes the way we communicate with Him. Instead of barking orders at God, we relax and converse with Him, savoring our relationship as we enjoy the ride.

Freedom from Formulas

Saul sought the Lord's blessing for his decisions using the formulas prevalent in his day: a word from prophets, a message in a dream, or casting lots with the Urim. He was continually frustrated that the Lord did not answer him through these means, so he sought answers from God through those who seemed better connected with Him, particularly Samuel. The religious formulas were not working for Saul.

Likewise, when we feel frustrated, we seek answers from those who seem better connected with God. That's why whenever something works for one person we try to mass-produce it into something that we conclude must work for all. This explains the multitude of prayer formulas floating around the Christian community. Jan Johnson writes, "This sort of formula-based spirituality teaches us to follow other people's paths to God, rather than developing our own relationship with Him."[3]

We tend to want a recipe for success in every aspect of life. Yet if you've ever been to a chili cook-off, you know that there is a seemingly infinite number of recipes for chili. What works for one person—chili hot enough to cause a four-alarm fire—may not work for another person. What works for one person in his or her relationship with God may not be compatible with another's temperament and style. Thankfully, God relates to us as individuals, whether we are hot and spicy, mild and flavorful, or anywhere in between. There are no recipes for relationships, so we need to set ourselves free from formulas and build a relationship with the Creator who made each of us infinitely different.

The most elaborate prayer formula I've seen and tried was the hour of prayer set forth by Dick Eastman, the director of Change the World School of Prayer.[4] He believes that since

3. Jan Johnson, *Enjoying the Presence of God: Discovering Intimacy with God in the Daily Rhythms of Life* (Colorado Springs, Colo.: NavPress, 1996), 18.
4. Dick Eastman, *The Hour That Changes the World: A Practical Plan for Personal Prayer* (Grand Rapids, Mich.: Baker Book House, 1978).

Jesus called upon His disciples to pray with Him for one hour (Matthew 26:40), that is the minimum acceptable time standard. Eastman divides an hour of prayer into five-minute segments and dedicates each of the twelve segments to a different aspect of prayer: praise, waiting, confession, Scripture praying, watching, intercession, petition, thanksgiving, singing, meditation, listening, and praise.

It is difficult to imagine Jesus praying like that. He never had a formulaic approach to God, and His request for the disciples to watch and pray for one hour was for a particular circumstance on the night of His betrayal. In John 17, Jesus essentially told God, "I've done what You sent Me to do. Now that I have to leave, protect My disciples and make them holy. And for future generations who believe, may they know that You love them like You love Me." That prayer is simple—no elaborate formulas.

Jesus provided an example of prayer (Matthew 6:9–13), not to provide a formula for prayer but to show us what our attitude should be as we converse with God. We are to acknowledge that God is in control ("Our Father who is in heaven, hallowed be Your name."), that we humbly submit to His will ("Your kingdom come, Your will be done, on earth as it is in heaven."), that we acknowledge our needs that only God can meet ("Give us this day our daily bread."), and that we seek forgiveness and help to live holy lives ("And forgive us our debts, as we also have forgiven our debtors. And do not lead us into temptation, but deliver us from evil."). These are not formulaic ingredients, but rather principles by which we can live in communion with God.

Brother Lawrence is known for his book, *The Practice of the Presence of God*, in which he describes how he trained himself to become aware of God's presence every moment of every day. He suggested that some forms of devotion should be laid aside "because these devotions are only means to attain to the end. So when by this exercise of the presence of God we are *with Him* who is our end, it is then useless to return to the means." He also advises, "Do not always scrupulously confine yourself to certain rules, or particular forms of devotion, but act with a general confidence in God, with love and humility."[5] In other words, focus on the relationship instead of the forms.

We do not use formulas for talking to our friends and family members. Dialogue with God should not be any different. Imagine telling your spouse over breakfast, "Okay, honey, I have twenty minutes. I'm going to spend five minutes telling you what a great spouse you are, five minutes telling you about the kids, five minutes telling you about what's going on at work, and five minutes telling you my plans for next weekend so I can do what I want with your blessing." Who talks to their spouse that way? There is no dialogue; the "conversation" is rigid and mechanical, and it lacks any of the warmth and genuineness of a healthy relationship. It sounds like a formula for a failure.

Our conversations with God should not be forced and unnatural; they should be a natural outflow of the relationship in the context of particular circumstances. We can talk to God—wherever we are, about whatever we think of—just as we would with any other person with whom we spend time.

5. Brother Lawrence, *The Practice of the Presence of God* (Uhrichsville, Ohio: Barbour and Company, Inc., 1993), 57, 59.

What's Love Got to Do with It?

Saul's relationship with God was mechanical, at best. He was going through the motions, but it's questionable whether he even loved God. Most believers would claim to love God, but, for many, their relationship with Him is governed by a mechanical series of exercises. A vigorous prayer regimen amounts to little more than mental exercise unless it is fueled by passion. Our heartfelt passion for God ought to saturate our thoughts and motivate our actions. After all, our passions dictate our pursuits.

Perhaps you've seen the diagram of the train with the engine, car, and caboose labeled *fact, faith*, and *feeling*. Many well-meaning believers teach that if facts (the truth of God's Word) drive the train engine, faith and those pesky, uncooperative feelings will follow. On the contrary, our feelings are what motivate us to action. Our love relationship is the basis of our faith:

> Our heartfelt passion for God ought to saturate our thoughts and motivate our actions.

"We love, because He first loved us" (1 John 4:19). Faith cannot be reduced to an act of the will, as if sheer determination will drag along our feelings until they catch up with our mental exercises.

People sometimes talk about the "twelve-inch gap" between their head and their heart, meaning that they know something but cannot translate it into a heartfelt belief. The implication, again, is that the head leads and the heart follows. Yet I only hear such references in conjunction with spiritual matters. In no other context is this head-leads-the-heart argument used to justify a lack of passion.

Think about something you are passionate about: sports, music, literature, politics, or a hobby. Did you first learn all you could and hope that eventually you would fall in love with this pursuit? Of course not. You were passionate about something, so you were motivated to study the facts. You wanted to get to know as much as possible about the thing for which you felt so much passion. The heart motivates our actions and shapes our beliefs.

We tend to treat our relationship with God like our relationship with a personal physician: We see Him periodically for a ten-minute appointment in which we present a list of circumstances or symptoms that we want Him to fix immediately, even miraculously. We want a quick-fix pill for everything.

In reality, most relationships are not maintained by a list of requests or demands on the other person. Such a relationship is doomed. What makes us think a list of prayer requests is the appropriate way to relate to God? Mulholland writes, "Our prayer tends to be a shopping list of things to be accomplished, an attempt to manipulate the symptoms of our lives without really entering into a deep, vital, transforming relationship with God."[6]

Remember being in love? You said, "I really love you—let's meet for breakfast every day for half an hour." No way! You wanted to spend every possible moment with that person. When you had to be apart for work and other responsibilities, you called several times a day just to say, "I can't get you off my mind." You spent as much time as possible together, sometimes without even exchanging words, just relaxing in each other's presence.

6. Mulholland, *Invitation to a Journey*, 105.

So which describes your relationship with God: a patient to a doctor or a beloved to a lover?

Discard Dutiful Devotions

Saul fulfilled his religious obligations out of a sense of duty and expected that formulas would produce the results he wanted, on command. Such tactics amount to little more than superstition. Saul even wanted to bring the ark of God into battle for a good-luck charm. You can't just do all the right things and expect to conjure up a particular result. God doesn't work like that. God desires devotion, not duty.

Devotion is not dedication. A person may be dedicated to a quiet time or devotional plan without being wholly devoted to God. Dedicated employees consistently give their time and effort to performing every assignment as required. However, dedicated employees may, nonetheless, hate their jobs. On the other hand, devoted employees give of their time and effort because their heart is in it. They are devoted to a cause larger than the individual tasks required of them, and that devotion motivates their exemplary work. Our devotion to God motivates us to spend increasing amounts of time with Him, though not necessarily through a disciplined schedule.

For too many Christians, quiet time, not God, has become the goal. They measure their spiritual life by their personal discipline rather than by the quality of their relationship. Missing this divine appointment is deemed a personal weakness—perhaps even a sin. Spending time with God is not about fulfilling a duty on a particular schedule; it's about a lifestyle that promotes good health in our relationship with Him.

Many guilt-ridden Christians, including the leaders of many churches, struggle to maintain a daily devotional regimen. This became evident to me while sitting around the fireplace one evening at a seminary prayer retreat. Student after student—future pastors and leaders—confessed their guilt and frustration at their inability to maintain a consistent and satisfying quiet time. But why the guilt? The guilt comes from feeling we have shirked our duty as Christians. Somewhere, somehow, spending time with God became a duty.

> Spending time with God is not about fulfilling a duty on a particular schedule; it's about a lifestyle that promotes good health in our relationship with Him.

Nurturing any relationship, especially with the One who loved me enough to die for me, should not be perceived as a duty that breeds guilt. Relationships based on guilt are unhealthy. What if your spouse said, "I promise to be a loyal spouse and spend ten minutes a day talking to you, but my goal is to gradually work up to twenty, and then thirty, minutes a day"; then, he started a timer, talked until the buzzer went off, and left with a sigh of relief that the burdensome task was done for another day? God doesn't want us to feel duty bound to spend time with Him.

Devotions are a matter of discipline; *devotion* is a matter of desire. After this distinction became clear to me, I quit my quiet time as a daily discipline. Suddenly, I began to spend more time with God than ever before because my focus changed from fulfilling a duty to building a relationship. I wasn't spending time with God because I had to, but because I wanted to, more than ever.

Take God Out of the Box

You could keep a puppy in a cage. After all, a puppy makes messes, so if he's in a cage, you have control over where he makes a mess. It's all contained, convenient, and controlled. For thirty minutes a day, you pet him and talk to him, and the puppy lavishes his wholehearted devotion on you with a bit of slobber. Okay, time's up—back in the cage until tomorrow. If you keep a puppy in a cage, you miss out on his constant companionship and lifelong loyalty. Sure it gets messy sometimes, but don't the joys outweigh the risks?

Perhaps we tend to keep God in a box like a puppy in a cage. That way we have control over how much of our lives He can mess with. It's all contained, convenient, and controlled. For thirty minutes a day, you open the box to pet Him and talk to Him, and He lavishes His wholehearted devotion on you. Then, time's up—back in the box until tomorrow.

If you keep God in a box, you miss out on His constant companionship, lifelong loyalty, and lavish love. Sure, life gets messy sometimes, but don't the joys outweigh the risks?

Saul did not integrate his relationship with God into all aspects of his life. His prayer life was a mere compartment of his entire life. He essentially kept God in a box, to be pulled out when he wanted God's approval for his plans.

The fallacy of a quiet time lies in restricting our interaction with God to a set block of time, leaving the remainder of the day to us. In this mentality, I'm still in control, like Saul, but I set aside time to seek the approval of my co-pilot. Mulholland makes the observation that "As long as God is perceived as 'out there,' separated from us, we understand ourselves as independent, autonomous beings."[7] In reality, the Holy Spirit resides within the believer. God is not "out there"; He is ever present. Restricting our interaction with God to a set block of time is unnatural. In fact, nowhere does the Bible even say to have a quiet time. The biblical model is to spend every moment of every day with God.

People scoff at 1 Thessalonians 5:17, where Paul writes that we are to "pray without ceasing," or try to explain it away: "Surely the Bible can't mean to pray without ceasing." People restrict God to a once-a-day plan, thinking that's more realistic. Yet in practice it is more difficult to meet the obligation of a daily quiet time without failure than it is to spend time with God at every possible moment throughout the day. Snippets of time with God here and there develop the intimacy that would occur in any other relationship in which you share an increasing number of experiences together. These moments together create a longing for more, and you look forward to when your schedule will allow you to spend extended time together. It's a natural development called intimacy.

Would you rather have an appointment with disappointment, or develop the intimacy that you long for? Let's explore these concepts more fully.

7. Mulholland, *Invitation to a Journey*, 95.

AN APPOINTMENT
WITH DISAPPOINTMENT

1. In terms of spending time with God, what works for you? What doesn't work? How do you feel about the quality of your prayer life?

   _____

   _____

   _____

   _____

   Saul: "The Lord Did Not Answer Him"

2. What was Saul's spiritual condition (1 Samuel 10:9–10; 1 Samuel 11:6)?

   _____

   _____

   _____

   _____

3. Yet how does the Bible describe Saul's interaction with God—his prayer life (1 Samuel 14:37; 1 Samuel 28:6; 1 Samuel 28:15)?

   _____

   _____

   _____

   _____

Who's in Charge Here?

4. Saul was frustrated that God did not answer him because that was the one element that Saul could not control. If you were to give God control of your life, how might it change the way you communicate with Him?

_____

_____

_____

Freedom from Formulas

5. In Saul's attempt to communicate with God, what three religious formulas did he try (1 Samuel 28:6)?

   1. _____

   2. _____

   3. _____

6. The religious formulas were not working for Saul. What formulas have you used for talking to God? Did they work for you?

_____

_____

_____

What's Love Got to Do with It?

7. Describe how we tend to treat our relationship with God like our relationship with a personal physician.

_____

_____

_____

_____

8. Describe how our relationship might be if we approached God as our Lover.

_____

_____

_____

Discard Dutiful Devotions

9. Devotions are a matter of discipline; devotion is a matter of desire. Explain the difference in your own words.

_____

_____

_____

10. Why is discipline or duty an inadequate basis for a relationship? How would you feel if someone spent time with you for the sake of duty?

_____

_____

_____

Take God Out of the Box

11. The fallacy of a quiet time lies in our restricting our interaction with God to a set block of time, leaving the remainder of the day to us. Nowhere in the Bible does it say to have a quiet time. What is the biblical model (1 Thessalonians 5:17)?

_____

_____

_____

_____

12. Would you rather have an appointment with disappointment or develop the intimacy that you long for with God? From what you've learned so far, how might that intimacy be possible?

_____

_____

_____

_____

two

A Man's Best Friend

*I*n many relationships, even peer-to-peer relationships, people settle into roles. One person often looks up to the other person, who usually leads, initiates, and encourages. While there might be a mutual giving in the relationship, there are also subtle roles, and when those roles are altered, the relationship is changed. This is evident in a parent-child relationship when, due to age, injury, or illness, roles are reversed and the child must care for the parent.

Jesus was the master and teacher over His disciples. The disciples' shock when Jesus washed their feet (John 13:5–17) illustrates their understanding of the role Jesus had in their relationship: He was superior, yet here He was taking on an inferior role. It made the disciples uncomfortable and disrupted their perception of their relational roles. Jesus went on to tell them, "I no longer call you servants, but friends" (John 15:15, paraphrased). Their roles were indeed changing, as their relationship was growing more intimate. The Upper Room Discourse (John 13–17) is the most intimate discussion Jesus had with the disciples.

Jesus, God Himself, calls you friend (John 15:14). Do you likewise call Him Friend? Are you willing to go to the next level in your relationship and experience a newer, deeper intimacy than perhaps you ever thought was possible?

The Bible says that God used to speak to Moses "just as a man speaks to his friend" (Exodus 33:11). Let's examine the relationship that Moses had with God and discover what it means to live our lives with an all-powerful, ever-present Friend.

Moses: "Just as a Man Speaks to His Friend"

Yahweh. God said His name was Yahweh. I AM WHO I AM. Moses mulled over his encounter with God at the burning bush, as he had so many times before. So much had happened since then: God sent Moses back to Egypt, and after a series of confrontations with Pharaoh and ten miraculous works of God against the Egyptians, Yahweh led His people out of captivity. Now, as dusk mediated between daylight and darkness, Yahweh's guiding presence was changing from a pillar of cloud to a pillar of fire. It was the pillar of fire that reminded Moses of the burning bush. *God's name is Yahweh.*

Three months later, after the Israelites had left the land of Egypt, the fire of God descended upon Mount Sinai, and Yahweh summoned Moses to the top of the mountain. There He gave Moses the laws governing the civil, moral, and religious practices of the new nation. Moses remained on the mountain for forty days and forty nights. Then, the anger of Yahweh was kindled against the people, for they had rebelled and formed a golden idol. Yahweh wanted to destroy the people, but Moses reminded Him that the Egyptians would believe that He brought His people into the wilderness to destroy them. So Yahweh changed His mind.

Moses returned to the camp and found the Israelites worshiping a golden calf. He confronted them for their great sin, and the next day he returned to Yahweh to confess, "The people have sinned by making a god of gold. If You will, forgive their sin. If not, please blot me out from Your book."

Yahweh said, "I will blot out whoever has sinned, but go now and lead the people to the land flowing with milk and honey. I will not go up with you, lest I destroy the people on the way, for they are an obstinate people."

Moses descended from the mountain in haste. When he told the people these things, they were grieved.

Moses used to pitch a tent outside the camp, and he called it the tent of meeting. Whenever Moses entered the tent, the pillar of cloud would descend upon it, and Yahweh would speak to Moses face to face, just as a man speaks to his friend.

Speaking as a friend now, Moses said to Yahweh, "You want me to lead these people, but You have not told me whom You will send with me. If I have found favor in Your sight, let me know Your ways that I may know You."

God replied, "My presence will go with you."

Moses thought a moment and then spoke carefully, "It is Your presence with us that distinguishes us from all other people on the earth. Without it, how will others know that we have found favor in Your sight?"

"I will do as you have asked, for you have found favor in My sight, Moses, and I have known you by name," God answered.

Moses felt emboldened by the vote of confidence and nearly shouted, "I ask You then, show me Your glory."

Yahweh said, "I will make My goodness pass before you and proclaim the name of Yahweh before you, but you cannot see My face. No one can see Me and live. Even so, I will hide you in the cleft of the rock and cover you with My hand until I have passed by. Then I will remove My hand so you can see My back, but you cannot see My face."

The next morning, while the faint glow of dawn gave hope to a new day, Moses climbed the familiar path to the top of Mount Sinai, with hope of his own that he would see the glory of God as Yahweh had promised. As always, Yahweh descended upon the mountain in the cloud and stood there with Moses. Then, Yahweh passed by in front of him and proclaimed, "I AM compassionate, gracious, patient, abounding in constant love and truth, forgiving rebellion, perversion, and sin; yet I will punish those who are guilty."

Moses bowed down to worship Yahweh. He pleaded, "Go with us, even though the people are so obstinate. Pardon our rebellion and sin and claim us as Your own."

"Go with us, even though the people are so obstinate. Pardon our rebellion and sin and claim us as Your own."

"Your people will see the work of Yahweh," answered God. "I will perform miracles that have never been seen in all the earth."

Moses stayed on Mount Sinai with Yahweh for forty days and forty nights. When he descended from the mountain, the skin of his face shone because he had been speaking with Yahweh face to face.

The people of Israel were afraid to come near Moses because his face shone. After Moses commanded them to obey everything that Yahweh had spoken, Moses put a veil over his face. Whenever he went before Yahweh, he would take off the veil. Afterwards, he would come out to instruct the people with his face shining, and then he would replace the veil until the next time he spoke to Yahweh.

A First-Name Basis

From his initial encounter with God at the burning bush, Moses was on a first-name basis with Yahweh.[1] To say that you are on a first-name basis with someone means that a relationship is developing. The relationship has progressed beyond formal acknowledgments to a more casual acquaintance. A step towards greater intimacy has occurred.

God is not an impersonal force; He is personal and relational. God revealed Himself to Moses by giving him His name, Yahweh, meaning I AM. Nothing is more personal than someone's name, and to the Hebrew mind, a name revealed a person's character. Thus, people changed their name to signify a change in character (Abram became Abraham [Genesis 17:5]; Jacob became Israel [Genesis 32:28]; Simon became Peter [Matthew 16:17–18]).

Moses knew God by name, but he wanted to know God's character. When Moses said, "Let me know Your ways that I may know You" and "Show me Your glory," he was essentially asking God to reveal His character. At a moment of crisis, when Israel proved unfaithful and God was threatening to abandon His people, Moses wanted to know: *What kind of God are you?*

Moses wanted a fuller knowledge of Yahweh and desired a deeper intimacy with Him. When Yahweh passed by, He proclaimed His name. The I AM described Himself as "compassionate and gracious, slow to anger, and abounding in loving-

1. The written form of Hebrew contained only consonants, and the name *YHWH* was generally not pronounced at all, for fear of profaning the holy name of God (Exodus 20:7). Therefore, we cannot be certain of the pronunciation, but it is generally accepted as Yahweh. Common practice became substituting the word *Adonai* (Lord) for YHWH in reverence for the divine name. In modern translations, YHWH appears as Lord (small caps) to distinguish it from Adonai, or Lord.

kindness and truth; who keeps lovingkindness for thousands, who forgives iniquity, transgression and sin; yet He will by no means leave the guilty unpunished, visiting the iniquity of fathers on the children and on the grandchildren to the third and fourth generations" (Exodus 34:6–7).

Through our dialogue with God, we can know God by name. We can learn of God's character as we increasingly share life's experiences with Him. We initially gain knowledge of God through His written word, but over time we also gain firsthand knowledge of His love, forgiveness, grace, patience, and compassion as we see God's character for ourselves. After Job's encounter with God, he prayed, "I have heard of You by the hearing of the ear; but now my eye sees You" (Job 42:5). In other words, we can hear about God, read about God, and know about God, but none of that can replace the kind of knowledge we gain from firsthand experience with God.

> Through our dialogue with God, we can know God by name. We can learn of God's character as we increasingly share life's experiences with Him.

The same is true in our relationships with others. We can know about someone, but we do not really know that person until we have a personal relationship with him or her over a period of time. Shared experiences help us to truly know the other person. For example, we can learn about God's character from how He interacted with Moses: God does not abandon His people, even when they rebel against Him. However, we do not personally know God's character until we learn that God does not abandon us when we have rebelled against Him. Firsthand experience is the only way to develop intimacy.

Being on a first-name basis with someone goes both ways. Not only did Moses know God by name, God also knew Moses by name. It might seem obvious that God knows our names, but remember that being on a first-name basis means a relationship is developing. When Yahweh told Moses, "I have known you by name" (Exodus 33:17), He was expressing His ongoing relationship with Moses. God was easing Moses' fear that He would sever their relationship and send Moses off on his own to lead the people without His presence.

God also knows us by name. He knew us before we were formed in the womb (Psalm 139:13–16), and He knows all about us, even down to the number of hairs on our head (Matthew 10:30). God knows us personally, yet He longs for a deeper relationship with each of us. He wants to know and be known on a first-name basis.

The Role of Prayer

What is the role of communication in any relationship? While at times we may communicate our needs and desires, most of our communication reflects the joy of shared experience. As we share experiences of happiness and pain, we strengthen our common bonds. We cannot expect immediate intimacy in the early stages of a relationship, but in the process of building the relationship, we gradually share deeper and more personal information with each other. Our relationship with God grows in similar fashion.

Moses had a relationship with God that was uniquely personal. The Bible says, "The LORD used to speak to Moses face to face, just as a man speaks to his friend" (Exodus 33:11). Although we do not speak to God face to face, our relationship with Him can be just as personal. We can develop a relationship with God in which we communicate, "just as a man speaks to his friend."

God is not a vending machine; we can't just put in our request with a dollar's worth of prayer and expect a tangible result to pop out. Our relationships with others do not work that way. We do not make constant demands on others, expecting immediate results. If we have a bad day at work and come home to tell our spouses or best friends all about it, do we expect them to fix it? No, we expect them to listen with empathy, without producing any results. We build a relationship with others, and part of that is being able to communicate openly about anything that happens in our lives, good or bad. Likewise, we need to understand that we can pour out our hearts to God without demanding Him to fix everything.

That's why it is important to understand the role of prayer. Prayer is primarily relational, not functional. Our purpose in approaching God should not be to achieve results by getting God to fulfill our demands, but rather to enjoy an intimate relationship with Him. Jan Johnson reminds us: "Our task, then, is to seek to know God not because we're hoping for dazzling answers, but because we love Him."[2]

Practices such as keeping a prayer list reflect a functional view of prayer, and this is consistent with an "appointment mentality" that says, "I will talk to God about these things when it is time to talk to God." Why not just talk to God about whatever comes up, whenever it comes up? Whenever a thought occurs to you that you need to talk to God about, just do it. Keeping a prayer list is like writing down a list of ailments to present to your doctor during your periodic ten-

2. Johnson, *Enjoying the Presence of God*, 95.

minute appointment. This functional view of prayer focuses on results rather than building a relationship in which we can freely discuss anything with our Lover, Jesus. Mother Teresa made this observation: "We complicate prayer as we complicate many things. It is to love Jesus with undivided love."[3]

Let me share a very personal example that illustrates what I mean when I say that the purpose of prayer is relational, not functional. When bouts of loneliness set in, I could pray that God would let me find someone special to marry. That would be a very functional, or results-oriented, prayer. Yet God knows the future; He knows whether I will ever get married. No amount of asking will change that. Instead, when faced with the dull ache of loneliness, I pray that God would draw me into such an intimate relationship with Him that I would find my contentment with Him until such time as He sees fit to give me over to an earthly husband.

If I had a functional view of prayer, it would be easy to spend years asking for a husband and to view those years as a personal or spiritual failure for my inability to prevail upon God to grant my request. However, with a relational view of prayer, success and failure become irrelevant. It's not a matter of prevailing upon God to serve me. I can trust Him and ask for what He is always willing to give: more of Himself.

Longing for More

The more we know God, the more we want to know God. Moses knew God's name, and he spoke with God face to face, as a man speaks to his friend. Yet Moses still pleaded, "Let

3. Mother Teresa, *Words to Love By . . .* , large print ed. (New York: Phoenix Press, Walker and Company, 1984), 44.

me know Your ways that I may know You," and "Show me Your glory." Moses desired deeper intimacy with God.

Any healthy relationship will grow increasingly intimate. Over time, we know each other more fully. We get past the superficial knowledge and know each other in ways that really matter. The same is true in our relationship with God. Over time, we know Him more fully, and yet the more we know Him, the more we desire to know Him.

Prayer, our dialogue with God, can be just as lively and "real" as our conversations with anyone else. Still, we cannot flip a switch and go from God-doesn't-seem-real-to-me to twenty-four-hour-a-day-intimacy.

I used to find it difficult to converse with a Being that didn't have skin. I wanted someone I could touch or hug. I simply wanted to see the understanding look in my Listener's eyes as I shared my heart. However, the more experiences I had with God, the more I discovered how real He is. The joys of intimacy with God are immensely satisfying—more satisfying than measuring my "success" at getting God to answer a list of requests.

> The joys of intimacy with God are immensely satisfying—more satisfying than measuring my "success" at getting God to answer a list of requests.

Moses knew God intimately and asked for more of God. The Lord did allow Moses to see Him in a new way, but He allowed Moses only as much as he could handle. When Moses asked God to reveal more of Himself, the Lord replied, "You cannot see My face, for no man can see Me and live!" (Exodus 33:20). However, God gave Moses only a glimpse of His glory: "You shall see My back, but My face shall not be seen" (Exodus 33:23). As we seek more in our relationship with God, He will give us as much of Himself as we can handle at the moment.

Unlimited Talk Time

Whenever Moses entered the tent of meeting, the presence of God would settle upon it in a cloud. God apparently had an open-door policy with Moses: Whenever Moses wanted to talk, God was ready to listen. Since Moses was on a first-name basis with God, he essentially had a family-and-friends plan with unlimited talk time. Moses would enter God's presence and fellowship with Him continually for as long as forty days. His face-to-face communication with God was only broken when God gave Moses a task to accomplish, which generally meant he had to leave the physical presence of God to do it.

For believers today, the Holy Spirit resides within us, so we cannot leave God's presence. Yet our awareness of God's presence can be developed into increasing periods of fellowship. We also have a family-and-friends plan with unlimited talk time, but too often we do not take advantage of the offer. God extends His offer of continual fellowship and unlimited communication, but we often seem content with an occasional brief chat.

So what did Moses and Yahweh talk about for forty days at a time? They dialogued about the details of leading God's people through the wilderness. Together, they resolved many problems, decided upon appropriate courses of action, and administered the details of establishing a national legal system and religious structure. Yet their communication was not primarily functional; it was relational. Moses was always concerned about protecting God's reputation, so that Egypt and the other nations would not have cause to say that God brought His people into the wilderness to destroy them or that God was unable to bring them to the Promised Land. Similarly, God was always concerned with relieving the burden of leadership for Moses. Any relationship characterized by mutual concern is not a relationship focused on using the other person to achieve specific results.

Moses communicated with God in ways that were open and transparent. The fact that he removed the veil whenever he entered God's presence indicates that there was nothing between Moses and God. Moses had nothing to hide. God knew him completely, and Moses felt free to come to God just as he was, whether depressed and discouraged (Numbers 11:10–15), angry (Numbers 16:15), joyful (Exodus 15), fatigued (Exodus 17:10–12), frustrated (Exodus 5:22–23), concerned (Numbers 12:13), or remorseful (Exodus 32:31–32; Numbers 14:19). Likewise, God conveyed His feelings to Moses, expressing anger (Exodus 32:9–10; Numbers 14:11–12), concern (Exodus 19:20–25), disgust (Exodus 33:1–3), compassion (Exodus 33:19–23), and hope (Exodus 34:10). Conveying such emotions characterizes communication that is relational, not functional.

As our relationship with God grows more intimate, we will discover much more to talk about than our list of requests. Our communication will become more personal and relational. We will begin to use more minutes of our unlimited talk time.

Relationships Change Us

Think back over your past relationships. If you have had a close relationship with someone, you may have discovered that over time, the two of you probably began to talk alike, look alike, or think alike. Perhaps you reached a point where you could finish each other's sentences. Beyond these superficial qualities, a significant relationship probably changed you at a deeper level. An adverse relationship may have made you more guarded, defensive, angry, or bitter. A positive relationship may have made you more patient, kind, forgiving, loving, or sensitive. There is no doubt that relationships change us.

Meeting with God face to face changed Moses' appearance: His face glowed! The glory of God was reflected on his face in a way that astonished others. How much more then, with God indwelling our lives, should our countenances reflect the glory of God? The apostle Paul wrote, "But we all, with unveiled face, beholding as in a mirror the glory of the Lord, are being transformed into the same image from glory to glory, just as from the Lord, the Spirit" (2 Corinthians 3:18). Just as Moses' countenance was changed by God's presence, our countenance can be changed by God's presence.

Our countenances are like spiritual complexions, revealing the health of our spirits in the same way our physical complexions reveal the health of our bodies. Believe it or not, there is a significant change in our spiritual complexions as a result of the work of God's grace in our lives. As the relaxed glow of God's peace radiates from our being, people will notice the difference.

> There is a significant change in our spiritual complexions as a result of the work of God's grace in our lives. As the relaxed glow of God's peace radiates from our being, people will notice the difference.

I used to be angry, fearful, and guarded in my relationships, even during my first few years as a Christian. Eventually, I forgave others and trusted God to protect my relationships. Once this transformation began, my ability to relate to those around me was transformed in a matter of months. During that time, at least half a dozen people told me that my countenance had changed. They described it in different ways, saying that I looked happier or more relaxed or that they could see in my face that I was in the center of God's will. I was thrilled by the feedback but also a bit mystified. I couldn't see the difference. Apparently, the change had been impressive enough for people to actually tell me they noticed the difference.

Relationships change us, especially our relationship with a holy, all-powerful God.

A MAN'S BEST FRIEND

1. In John 15:14–15, Jesus was explaining how His relationship with the disciples was changing. What change was happening?

   _____

   _____

   _____

2. Do you think of God as your best friend? How do you want your relationship with God to change?

   _____

   _____

   _____

Moses: "Just As a Man Speaks to His Friend"

3. As we discussed in chapter one, how did God respond to Saul? By contrast, how did God respond to Moses? (See 1 Samuel 28:15; Exodus 33:11.)

   _____

   _____

   _____

   _____

A First-Name Basis

4. God is not an impersonal force; He is personal and relational. When He passed by Moses, He proclaimed

His name. What did God give as His name (Exodus
34:6–7)?

_____

_____

_____

_____

5. We can hear about God, read about God, and know
   about God, but none of that can replace the kind of
   knowledge we gain from firsthand experience with
   God. Give an example of a time you learned something about God through firsthand experience.

_____

_____

_____

_____

_____

6. What did God tell Moses, and what does He tell us,
   in these verses?

   Exodus 33:17:

_____

_____

   Psalm 139:13–16:

_____

_____

   Matthew 10:30:

_____

_____

The Role of Prayer

7. What is the role of communication in any relationship?

_____

_____

_____

_____

_____

_____

8. The purpose of prayer is primarily relational, not functional. Give an example of a functional view of prayer. Give an example of a relational view of prayer.

_____

_____

_____

_____

_____

_____

Longing for More

9. Moses knew God intimately and asked for more of God. Write out a prayer indicating your desire to know God more intimately. Use a separate sheet of paper if necessary.

_____

_____

_____

_____

_____

Unlimited Talk Time

10. For believers today, the Holy Spirit resides within us. Our awareness of God's presence can be developed into increasing periods of fellowship. Write down three times of day when you will start conversing with God (for example, while folding laundry, while in the shower, and while doing dishes).

1. _____
   _____
   _____

2. _____
   _____
   _____

3. _____
   _____
   _____

11. Moses felt free to come to God just as he was. From the list below, circle the condition that you identify with most right now and look it up. Then talk to God about how you feel.

Depressed and discouraged (Numbers 11:10–15)

Angry (Numbers 16:15)

Joyful (Exodus 15)

Fatigued (Exodus 17:10–12)

Frustrated (Exodus 5:22–23)

Concerned (Numbers 12:13)

Remorseful (Exodus 32:31–33:2; Numbers 14:19)

Relationships Change Us

12. Give an example of how a past relationship changed you. How might a relationship with a holy, all-powerful God change you?

_____

_____

_____

_____

Supplicate or Suffocate

$\mathcal{S}$upplication. It's not a word we use in everyday conversation, but we are familiar with the concept. A beggar asking for help is a suppliant, one who is needy and requests help from someone who is able to meet that need.

The Seattle area, where I grew up, is a haven for homeless people because of the mild winters. As you walk the streets of downtown, panhandlers call out to you, extending their hands, expecting a handout, with the hope that they will receive what they have requested. Like those Seattle panhandlers, we can have the same confidence toward God, for Jesus promised that those who ask would receive (Matthew 7:8).

A prayer of supplication presents a need to God and makes a humble, earnest request that God meet that need. Suppliants acknowledge their inability to meet their own needs and believe that God is able to meet those needs. Supplication, therefore, expresses our total dependence on God.

Nehemiah's life was characterized by supplication. Whether he faced a monumental crisis or everyday nuisances, he expressed each need to God. Let's see what we can learn from this humble suppliant who took bold action.

Nehemiah: "Our God Will Fight for Us"

"Hanani!" exclaimed Nehemiah, throwing his arms around his brother, whom he had not seen in years. "How was your journey? Are you well? And your family? How is the city of our God after all these years? How much reconstruction has taken place? Tell me, brother. You must tell me everything."

"Of course," chuckled Hanani, "I will tell you all that you wish to hear and more, as soon as you cease assaulting me with questions."

As Hanani began to deliver news of family and friends, the two men strolled down a long corridor elaborately decorated in fine silk and gold ornaments, for this was the palace of Artaxerxes, king of Persia.

"Yes, yes, Nehemiah, do not stare at me with your mouth agape. Your little niece, my daughter Sarah, is grown and married now. She married a farmer, but it is a struggle for them, as it is for all of us." Hanani paused to let that sink in, and then continued in a more solemn tone, "Now that I have told you all the news that you wished to hear, I must tell you more that you do not wish to hear."

"Go on," urged Nehemiah, reluctantly.

"The people of Jerusalem are distressed and disgraced. The wall of the city is broken down, and its gates are burned with fire."

"Again?" asked Nehemiah, a bit puzzled.

Hanani nodded, cleared his throat, and continued, "As you know, years ago, Cyrus, king of Persia, liberated our people from Babylon and allowed them to return to Jerusalem to rebuild the temple. Despite constant opposition, work progressed quickly. Our adversaries sent letters of complaint, but Cyrus' successor, King Darius, permitted us to continue work on the temple. After the temple was completed, the laborers set to work rebuilding the city walls. Once again, our enemies sent letters of complaint to the present king, Artaxerxes, whom you serve. They convinced the king that if the walls were restored, the people would declare their independence and no longer pay taxes to the king, having a position from which to defend the city from the Persian army. Therefore, King Artaxerxes issued an order for them to stop work, which our enemies zealously enforced by burning the walls and gates that the laborers were rebuilding."

Nehemiah gasped in disbelief, clenched his fists, and paced a circle around his brother, who now stood on the portico. Flushed with anger, Nehemiah fell to his knees and wept. From that point, nothing Hanani said would comfort his brother. Hanani stayed with his brother at his official residence on the palace grounds, but Nehemiah was despondent for days—fasting, weeping, praying, and nearly forgetting his guest, who had traveled more than a thousand miles to see him.

> Humbled by the enormity of the situation, yet confident in God's ability and power, Nehemiah knelt in supplication.

Four months elapsed since Hanani told Nehemiah the news of Jerusalem, and now the king had returned to his winter palace in Susa, and Nehemiah had to return to his duties. He knew what he must do today, but he was afraid. The king had issued a stop-work order in Jerusalem, but Nehemiah must ask the king to reconsider that order.

Humbled by the enormity of the situation, yet confident in God's ability and power, Nehemiah knelt in supplication: "O Lord, listen to my earnest prayer and make Your servant successful today and grant Your servant compassion before this man." With that, Nehemiah clothed himself for duty as the king's official cupbearer.

As Nehemiah took up the wine and presented it to the king, Artaxerxes asked, "Why is your face sad?"

Nehemiah cautiously responded, "The place of my fathers' tombs lies desolate, and the city gates have been consumed by fire." Nehemiah knew the Persian kings viewed tombs as sacred ground, and he hoped to evoke some compassion by carefully phrasing his response.

"What is your request?" asked the king.

Nehemiah breathed a prayer as he drew a long, slow, deep breath. "If it pleases the king, send me to Judah."

"How long will you be gone?" asked the king, who smiled slightly when he saw Nehemiah sigh with relief.

Nehemiah gave the king a definite time for his return, and the king provided Nehemiah with official travel documents and an armed escort, for the king had appointed Nehemiah to be governor in the land of Judah.

When Nehemiah arrived in Jerusalem, he rode around the city wall under cover of darkness, surveying the damage and appraising the repair work needed. Then, he gathered the officials of Jerusalem and said, "Come, let us rebuild the wall of Jerusalem." The leaders of Jerusalem agreed and began to help rebuilding the wall.

Foreigners were angry that the repairs were in progress. Sanballat and Tobiah, the leaders of their adversaries, inquired of Nehemiah, "King Artaxerxes issued a stop-work order. Are you rebelling against the king?"

"You foreigners have no claim to Jerusalem, and as for the rebuilding, our God will give us success," replied Nehemiah.

Sanballat and Tobiah continued to ridicule them and oppose their work. "Look at what they are doing!" they cried out for the builders to hear. "They think they can bring that heap of rubble back to life, but those stones are so badly burned that if a fox climbed up on them, they would break to pieces!"

The people worked diligently until the wall was restored to half its height, but they became tired and discouraged. They tried to salvage the materials, but the limestone was so badly burned that many of the stones were cracked, and some of it was completely disintegrating. The workers complained, "There is too much rubble to rebuild the wall."

Nehemiah knew that the people were overwhelmed, not by the task, for they had made so much progress already, but by the criticism of their enemies. Nehemiah therefore prayed: "We are despised by our enemies, Lord. They continually insult us, but actually they are insulting You. So let their insults bounce off of us and deflect back onto them."

When their insults did not slow the progress, the foreigners conspired to fight against Jerusalem. The Jews heard of their plan and were afraid. Nehemiah and the others with him prayed that God would help them overcome the obstacles and disruptions of their adversaries. He then stationed entire families on the wall together, with half of them working and the other half watching and protecting with spears. He encouraged them, saying, "Do not be afraid of them; remember the Lord and fight for your families. Our God will fight for us."

Their enemies continued to try to frighten and discourage the people so that they would give up. In the face of such opposition, Nehemiah could do nothing but remain dependent on God. He continually prayed, "O God, strengthen my hands."

After the wall was built, but before the gates were constructed, Sanballat wanted to meet with Nehemiah personally, but Nehemiah knew they only wanted to harm him, so he refused to leave his work. Then they tried to blackmail Nehemiah, saying that if he did not meet with them, they would report to Artaxerxes that he was plotting to revolt against the Persian king and appoint himself as king of Judah.

"You are just inventing these lies," replied Nehemiah, and he prayed for those who were trying to frighten him: "Lord, remember Tobiah and Sanballat for what they have done, for they are trying to intimidate me to keep me from accomplishing the work You have given me."

In fifty-two days the wall was completed. When the enemies of Jerusalem heard it, they lost their confidence and realized that God had indeed helped accomplish this task. Nonetheless, Tobiah continued to send letters to intimidate Nehemiah.

"Hanani, my brother," said Nehemiah, as they embraced in the courtyard of the governor's residence. "When you came to Susa to tell me that the king whom I serve had issued a stop-work order for the rebuilding of the walls and that our enemies had seized the opportunity to destroy the walls, I felt the situation was impossible. And yet by acknowledging our dependence on God and making supplication to the Lord Who is able to do the impossible, we stand here in a fortified city. Now, as the king appointed me governor over the land of Judah, I appoint you, Hanani, over the city of Jerusalem."

A Million Bucks

Not only did Nehemiah ask the king for a leave of absence, he also boldly asked the king to reverse his royal edict that had stopped work on the walls of Jerusalem. Nehemiah even had the audacity to ask the king to fund the building project! Before Nehemiah asked the king, he asked God. Nehemiah's humble supplication to the Lord gave him the faith and courage to act and ask boldly.

Jesus said we could ask for anything, and it would be done for us. *So if I ask for a million dollars, God will provide it? And if He doesn't, God doesn't keep His promises, so why should I ask Him for anything else?* Before we decide that God is a promise breaker, it's important that we look at the context of Jesus' words in John 15.

"Apart from Me you can do nothing," Jesus said (John 15:5), suggesting that we are as dependent on God as a branch is dependent on the tree. Jesus then promised, "If you abide in Me, and My words abide in you, ask whatever you wish, and it will be done for you" (John 15:7). Jesus was teaching one essential point: dependence on God. *Abiding* expresses dependence. In a state of dependence, our supplication will be answered. Remember, beggars or suppliants are dependent on help from someone who is able to meet their needs.

If we absolutely needed a million dollars and humbly pleaded with God to meet our dire need because there was no way we could come up with that kind of money from our own resources, and if it glorified God to do so, God would provide.

> When we humble ourselves before God, we are able to see His true greatness. He answers beyond our wildest dreams.

Nehemiah needed a million bucks, so to speak, and God provided. Nehemiah boldly asked the king for letters of safe passage and a letter of requisition for the timber to make beams for the gates: "And the king granted them to me because the good hand of my God was on me" (Nehemiah 2:8). Nehemiah humbly acknowledged that it was not the result of his great influence that the king donated these resources; it was the hand of God supplying a great need in response to supplication. God was glorified.

When we humble ourselves before God, we are able to see His true greatness. He answers beyond our wildest dreams. God "is able to do far more abundantly beyond all that we ask or think" (Ephesians 3:20). Each answer increases our faith in God's faithfulness.

Ready, Willing, and Able

Trust really amounts to having faith in God's faithfulness, as Nehemiah did. His statements of faith, such as "the God of heaven will give us success" (Nehemiah 2:20) or "Our God will fight for us" (4:20), indicate a wholehearted faith that God could and would meet the need of the moment. Do we really believe that God can and will meet our needs?

The first step toward trusting God is to believe that God is able to meet our needs. Nothing is impossible for Him. His ability and power are unlimited. It may seem as if God is restricted by human actions, as if He is unable to intervene, but He chooses to allow situations to unfold naturally, and His intervention occurs in the hearts of those who turn to Him as needy suppliants. Looking back on the painful experiences of my life, I can see that although God was able to prevent my pain, He proved Himself more faithful to me by demonstrating that He was able to heal my pain when I brought it to Him.

We must also trust that God is willing to meet our needs. Sometimes we ask for the healing of a loved one or some other request dear to our hearts, and when God does not grant our request, we wonder why God was not willing. He may not grant every request as we wish, but He will meet our need of the moment—whether it is grief, anxiety, or loneliness. As a loving Father, He longs to lavish His love on us. However, He waits patiently for us to come to Him. He loves us more than we can imagine and is willing to meet every need.

God knows our needs better than we do. Sometimes we don't really know what we need, but God does. God is always ready to answer, sometimes before we ask. In our moment of pain, in our darkest hour of doubt, in the depths of despair, God is there. Whenever we realize our need, we can instantly give it to Him because He is already there.

> In our moment of pain, in our darkest hour of doubt, in the depths of despair, God is there. Whenever we realize our need, we can instantly give it to Him because He is already there.

In the Bible, hope and trust are almost interchangeable concepts. Hope, in the biblical sense, is not wishful thinking; it is eager expectation. Bert Dominy writes, "Hope is the confidence that what God has done for us in the past guarantees our participation in what God will do in the future."[1] Knowing that God has worked in our lives in the past assures us that He will continue to do so in the future. Trust is built on experience (and experience is built on time spent with God).

The more we trust God, the more we will depend on Him; the more we depend on Him, the more we will trust Him. In this way we can learn to have faith in God's faithfulness. Trust is a matter of believing, as Nehemiah did, that "our God will fight for us."

1. Bert Dominy, "Hope," in *Holman Bible Dictionary,* ed. Trent C. Butler (Nashville, Tenn.: Holman, 1991), 665.

Humble Pie

Eventually, we will have more confidence in God's ability and power than in our own. Nehemiah's life was saturated with a humble acknowledgment that he was inadequate for the circumstances he encountered, but his humble supplication to the Lord gave him the faith and courage to act boldly.[2]

Paul expresses this same humble faith: "Such confidence we have through Christ toward God. Not that we are adequate in ourselves to consider anything as coming from ourselves, but our adequacy is from God" (2 Corinthians 3:4–5). It is humbling to admit that we are inadequate, but in order to assume the posture of a humble suppliant, we must acknowledge our inability to meet our needs.

The familiar imperative "Humble yourselves in the presence of the Lord" (James 4:10) may seem vague to modern readers. Pride is so deeply imbedded in our thinking that we can barely fathom what it means to humble ourselves. As an adjective, *humble* describes an attitude, but as a verb, *humble* is more than just an attitude; it is an action. So what must we do to humble ourselves? Wear sackcloth and throw ashes on our heads? To start, we can stop trying to control our lives, though breaking that habit may be more difficult than it appears.

2. For instance, King Artaxerxes had issued a stop-work order on the walls of Jerusalem. For Nehemiah to essentially ask his boss to reverse that order was a risky request. As cupbearer, he put his life on the line for the king, tasting the wine to ensure that it was not poisoned. By nature of the job, he was both trusted and expendable. As such, the king's response to this audacious request could go either way: trust Nehemiah or terminate him.

Control Freaks Anonymous

Supplication is the recovery program for the control freak in all of us. This addiction requires a lifetime of recovery, so repeat this phrase often: "Hi, my name is _____. I'm a control freak."

As control freaks, we must admit our inability to meet our needs and control our lives. In supplication we surrender control to God. Nehemiah bathed all his actions in prayer, surrendering control of his plans to God.

> Supplication is the recovery program for the control freak in all of us. This addiction requires a lifetime of recovery.

James understood that the control freak in each of us keeps us from approaching God as a needy suppliant seeking resources from above: "You lust and do not have; so you commit murder. You are envious and cannot obtain; so you fight and quarrel. You do not have because you do not ask" (James 4:2).

As control freaks, we are convinced that we know what's best for our lives. We fight for our "rights" at the expense of relationships. We feel we have a "right" to happiness, so whatever we think will make us happy seems worth a fight. We feel we have a "right" to justice, so we bring lawsuits against one another. We feel we have a "right" to respect—we feel underappreciated, underpaid, and overworked—so we climb over others on our way up the ladder of success. We think we deserve more; we deserve better. Our desire to control our lives and choose our destinies keeps us from submitting our requests to God. James says, "You do not have because you do not ask" (4:2).

We do not ask because we fear that God might say no. James addresses this point: "You ask and do not receive, because you ask with wrong motives, so that you may spend it on your pleasures" (4:3). Even in prayer, we try to control our lives by making demands on God for the outcome we think is best. Satisfying our ego drives us to control everything, even God.

Self-indulgent motives hinder our prayers, at least in the sense that we will not receive the things we seek in this manner. However, we are free to bring any request to God and submit our desires to Him. The difference is that we tend to approach God with closed fists, tightly clinging to our desires, pounding the table to make our demands. When we submit those desires to God in an openhanded manner, we allow God to change our desires rather than meet our demands. This is the relational benefit of prayer. Resigning control to God becomes a continual offering of our lives and our deepest desires to God.

James says, "God is opposed to the proud, but gives grace to the humble" (4:6). We can approach God proudly, with closed fists, but God will oppose us, and we will not receive what we ask for. Or we can approach God humbly, with open hands and an open heart, willing to receive what God has for us rather than whatever we think we want.

James speaks directly to the control freak in each of us: "Come now, you who say, 'Today or tomorrow we will go to such and such a city, and spend a year there and engage in business and make a profit.' Yet you do not know what your life will be like tomorrow. You are just a vapor that appears for a little while and then vanishes away. Instead, you ought to say, 'If the Lord wills, we will live and also do this or that'" (4:13–15). James squishes the pride of control by forcing us to admit that we cannot even control tomorrow. Instead, we are like the morning fog, which won't make it through the day, no matter how much it tries.

Although we must submit our plans to God, our hopes and desires are not irrelevant. Nehemiah desired to see God's city restored, and God used those hopes and dreams to accomplish it through someone who had a passion for the task. God often uses our hopes and dreams for His glory, but that can only happen when they are surrendered to Him. As long as we cling to our hopes and desires, God cannot use them, and we will only be frustrated in our efforts to achieve them apart from God.

Our boastful pride gets us nothing (James 4:3, 16), but if we humble ourselves before God, we will be exalted (James 4:10). God loves it when we admit our weakness and poverty before Him, not because He is on some ego trip but because He takes action when it will glorify His name to others. As Paul said, "We have this treasure in earthen vessels, so that the surpassing greatness of the power will be of God and not from ourselves" (2 Corinthians 4:7). God works through weak vessels so that He gets the credit.

Poor, But Not Beggars

Nehemiah prayed, "O God, strengthen my hands" (Nehemiah 6:9). In the face of opponents who were trying to discourage, threaten, and frighten him, Nehemiah prayed that fear would not weaken his hands. He recognized his physical and emotional weakness and asked God to work through him to accomplish the task. This humble dependence is characteristic of a suppliant.

God says that He dwells with the humble: "I dwell on a high and holy place, and also with the contrite and lowly of spirit in order to revive the spirit of the lowly and to revive the heart of the contrite" (Isaiah 57:15). God is near to those who express their need for Him. He says, "But to this one I will look, to him who is humble and contrite of spirit, and who trembles at My word" (Isaiah 66:2).

Jesus said, "Blessed are the poor in spirit" (Matthew 5:3). To be poor in spirit is to express our total dependence on God. Just as beggars live by asking, we are to live by asking, for Jesus promised that those who ask would receive (Matthew 7:8). Yet we are not beggars; we are God's children. The difference is that when beggars are needy and ask for help, they are desperate and despairing; but children simply trust that a loving father will meet every need, whether realized or not.

Jesus said (Matthew 7:7–11) that if humans naturally give good gifts to their children, "How much more will your Father who is in heaven give what is good to those who ask Him!" (v. 11). Likewise, John exclaimed, "See how great a love the Father has bestowed on us, that we would be called children of God; and such we are" (1 John 3:1). God loves His children and longs to lavish His love on us. When we extend our hands to Him, we are not begging; rather, we are receiving what a loving Father has to give us in response to our supplication.

> When we extend our hands to Him, we are not begging; rather, we are receiving what a loving Father has to give us in response to our supplication.

Perhaps David understood this when he wrote, "Hear the voice of my supplications when I cry to You for help, when I lift up my hands toward Your holy sanctuary" (Psalm 28:2). When David extended his hands to God in supplication, he expected God to extend His hand back in mercy.[3] Beggars—in the midst of their need—extend their hands to passers-by, indicating their expectation that the one they are entreating is able and willing to meet that need. David believed that God would respond favorably to his humble supplication and declared his confident hope: "Blessed be the LORD, because He has heard the voice of my supplication. The LORD is my strength and my shield; my heart trusts in Him, and I am helped" (vv. 6–7).

Breathe without Ceasing

Paul urges us to "pray at all times in the Spirit" (Ephesians 6:18). The word translated *pray* is the word for supplication. We are to make supplication in the Spirit, admitting our inability and God's ability to meet our needs. Paul also said, "Pray without ceasing" (1 Thessalonians 5:17). Some might say that to "pray at all times" simply means to pray frequently, but to "pray without ceasing" clearly refers to constant prayer. Is constant prayer even possible?

Some people would say no. They argue that we cannot "pray without ceasing" because we have to sleep. Yet, do you fear that you might cease to breathe if you fall asleep? Probably not. The rhythm of inhaling and exhaling carries on automatically. Likewise, the rhythm of communing with God carries on without any conscious thought. The Spirit within

3. Throughout the Bible, lifting the hands is a symbolic expression of dependence on God. The vigil of Moses while Joshua fought the Amalekites (Exodus 17:8–16) is one such example. Whenever Moses held his hands up, entreating the Lord's favor, Israel prevailed; whenever he put his hands down, Amalek prevailed. Another example occurred as Solomon prayed, in the dedication of the temple, that whenever someone reached out to God in supplication, God would respond according to the heart of the suppliant (1 Kings 8:38–39).

us knows our deepest needs and cries out to God without our awareness: "Because you are sons, God has sent forth the Spirit of His Son into our hearts, crying, 'Abba! Father!'" (Galatians 4:6).

In fact, Zechariah 12:10 refers to the Holy Spirit as "the Spirit of grace and of supplication." More than crying out to God, the Holy Spirit actually prays for us. Romans 8:26–27 says, "In the same way the Spirit also helps our weakness; for we do not know how to pray as we should, but the Spirit Himself intercedes for us with groanings too deep for words; and He who searches the hearts knows what the mind of the Spirit is, because He intercedes for the saints according to the will of God." So the role of the Spirit is to help our weakness through a ministry of supplication.

Naturally, God's Spirit within us knows our thoughts and feelings, as if our thoughts are actually prayers. Whether we realize it or not, we are continually communing with the Spirit who is ready, willing, and able to meet our needs.

Although God may be ready, willing, and able to meet our needs, we must be ready, willing, and able to stop trying to control our lives and ask for God's help. Paul says that true believers "worship in the Spirit . . . and put no confidence in the flesh" (Philippians 3:3). We cannot make a one-time decision to stop trying to control our lives and start depending on God. It becomes a continual process of surrendering control and receiving God's resources. As we stop trying to control our lives, we learn to depend on God. When He is proven trustworthy, we relinquish a bit more control of our lives. This positive cycle repeats itself, forming the rhythm by which we live and breathe.

> Stop trying to control my life (exhale).
> Depend on God (inhale).
> Stop trying to control my life (exhale).
> Depend on God (inhale).

The rhythm becomes so natural that we eventually stop concentrating on our breathing exercises. It becomes a sub-conscious, automatic function of life. So then prayer is not something we do once a day; prayer becomes the rhythm of our life. Each moment we choose to supplicate or suffocate.

SUPPLICATE OR SUFFOCATE

1. What is supplication?

_____

_____

_____

Nehemiah: "Our God Will Fight for Us"

2. How do these verses describe Nehemiah's dependence on God (Nehemiah 2:20; 4:20)?

_____

_____

_____

A Million Bucks

3. After making his requests to the king, to what did Nehemiah attribute his success (Nehemiah 2:7–8)?

_____

_____

_____

4. What can we do? What can God do (John 15:5; Ephesians 3:20)?

_____

_____

_____

_____

Ready, Willing, and Able

5. Do you believe that God can and will meet your needs? Give an example of how God has proved Himself faithful to you.

_____

_____

_____

6. Think of an area in which you need to trust God. Write out a prayer of supplication, expressing your need and your faith in God's ability to meet that need.

_____

_____

_____

Humble Pie

7. Describe the posture of a suppliant (James 4:10; 2 Corinthians 3:4–5).

_____

_____

_____

Control Freaks Anonymous

8. Even in prayer we try to control our lives by making demands on God for the outcome we think is best. Read James 4:1–17. What does it say about prayer and our attitudes?

_____

_____

_____

Poor, But Not Beggars

9. What qualities of a beggar does God desire in us (Matthew 5:3; Isaiah 57:15; Isaiah 66:2)?

_____

_____

_____

10. Why don't we need to beg for things from God (1 John 3:1; Matthew 7:7–11)?

_____

_____

_____

Breathe without Ceasing

11. What is the role of the Holy Spirit to help our weakness (Zechariah 12:10; Galatians 4:6; Romans 8:26–27)?

_____

_____

_____

12. In light of this, does it seem possible to pray without ceasing?

_____

_____

_____

God's Word to Me

*T*oo often we rush into God's presence, present our list of demands, and then rush out of God's presence just as hastily. Prayer should be a two-way conversation. We understand our side of the dialogue as we talk to God, but we must also take time to listen to Him. Listening to God begins with His written Word, the Bible. Since God communicates with us primarily through His written Word, it is important for us to eagerly immerse ourselves in it.

Mother Teresa underscored the significance of Scripture in our conversation with God when she said, "The beginning of prayer is scripture . . . We listen to God speaking." The implication is that listening to God is where the conversation begins. She goes on to describe the interactive nature of this two-way conversation: "And then we begin to speak to him again from the fullness of our heart. And he listens. That is really prayer. Both sides listening and both sides speaking."[1]

We already learned that our relationship with God ought to be more interactive than a half-hour appointment with Him. This interactive relationship begins with God's Word as

1. Mother Teresa, *Words to Love By . . .* , 38.

we listen to what He has to say to us, and then we respond in word and deed.

Let's peer into the life of Ezra, who is an example of one who studied the lessons of God's Word and applied them to life, both for himself and for others. From his experience, we can see what it means to interactively communicate with God through two-way conversation.

Ezra: "Set His Heart to Study the Law of the LORD and to Practice It"

Ezra concluded his speech with a boast: "The hand of our God acts favorably on behalf of those who seek Him." Ezra paused and continued more sternly, "But the hand of God exerts His power and anger against those who forsake Him." With these final words of admonishment, Ezra slowly took three steps backward and bowed at the waist to indicate deference to the king of Persia. His mind raced back through the contents of his presentation, and he silently questioned his own words: *What am I doing speaking so forcibly to the king of the most powerful kingdom in history?* Ezra slowly raised his head again when he heard the king clear his throat and begin to speak.

"Well then," said King Artaxerxes, "may it be so for you and anyone that chooses to go with you to Jerusalem. Within the hour you will have my royal decree and letter of credit, granting you authority to appoint local judges who know the laws of your God and ordaining you to teach the laws of your God to any who do not know them. Whatever the God of heaven has decreed, let it be done with diligence, and whoever does not obey the law of your God and the law of the king must be punished. Furthermore, since you say the hand of God exercises wrath upon those who forsake Him, I will make a royal offering for your temple, for I do not wish my kingdom to be a target of wrath for the God of heaven."

Ezra replayed the scene in his mind as he walked to the residential district to spread the word that the exiles were free to return to Jerusalem with him. It seemed as though his feet barely touched the ground. *Blessed be the Lord who has put all this in the king's heart. The Lord our God has extended favor to me before the king.* More than ever in his life, Ezra felt the hand of the Lord upon him.

After Ezra assembled all of the provisions, leaders, and volunteers who agreed to return to Jerusalem, they lingered at the river to fast and humble themselves before God to seek His protection for their journey. In Ezra's mind, God's reputation was at stake, for Ezra had boldly stated that God acts favorably toward those who seek Him. In light of this, how could Ezra have asked the king for a military escort for their journey? To do so would have indicated a lack of faith in God's favor toward His people. Yet if anything happened to them, God's reputation would be tarnished before the Persian leaders, for God would be deemed incapable of protecting them. No, God would protect them; God must protect them for His name's sake.

Four months and a thousand miles later, the refugees arrived in Jerusalem. Indeed, the hand of the Lord had been over them, delivering them from nationalistic enemies and highway bandits known to ambush weary travelers along the way.

When the refugees arrived in Jerusalem, they rested for three days. Although the people had been born in Babylon, sons and daughters of those who had been led into exile, they felt like they were home. Then they took an inventory of the provisions for the house of God: Everything had arrived safely. Together in the temple of their God, they sacrificed burnt offerings to the Lord.

Ezra and the leaders with him delivered the king's orders to the royal officers in the region. Though Ezra sensed some resistance from the officials at first, after they read the king's instructions they were willing to accommodate the refugees' requests in helping them settle in Jerusalem.

After the refugees had time to get situated in and oriented to their new living conditions, Ezra called for all the people of Israel to assemble together in Jerusalem at the Water Gate on the first day of the seventh month. For years, Ezra had set his heart on studying the law and practicing it at the temple of God in Jerusalem. Ezra was a scribe, and, as a descendant of Aaron, he was trained in the Law of Moses, so now he had been given the opportunity to realize his dream, his true calling. In order to fulfill his calling from God and his mandate from the king to teach God's statutes to all the people of Israel, Ezra resolved to begin by reading the book of the Law of Moses to the entire assembly.

A high wooden platform had been constructed for the occasion. Many of the people began to assemble the day before and camped in front of the platform to reserve a good location, but it didn't matter because all the people could see Ezra as he ascended to the top of the platform above them. Ezra was carrying the book of the Law of Moses, and as he opened the scroll, all the people stood up. He read from the scroll from daybreak until noon, and through it all, the people listened attentively. Then Ezra praised the Lord, and the people lifted their hands and shouted "Amen! Amen!" As one body, the people bowed down and worshipped the Lord.

Observing the mood of the people, Ezra and Nehemiah spoke together quietly while the people worshipped. Then they ascended the platform to address the crowd. The people had been weeping in remorse as they listened to God's words, but Ezra and Nehemiah instructed them not to mourn but to celebrate this sacred day and to spend the remainder of the day feasting and rejoicing. So they celebrated with great joy, because they now understood the words of the Lord.

This process continued day after day. As Ezra read from the book of the law of God, the people were eager to obey whatever they learned. When they heard about the feast of booths, the people went out and gathered branches to build makeshift shelters as they had been instructed in God's Word. So they celebrated the feast of booths for a week. On the twenty-fourth day, Ezra read from the book for a quarter of the day, and the people spent another quarter in confession and worship. The musicians stood on the stairs of the platform and led the people in praising the Lord and confessing their sins before God.

Then, Nehemiah and the leaders representing all the people signed and sealed an agreement binding upon all the people. Now that they understood the law of God given through Moses, they vowed to obey all of God's commands, regulations, and decrees.

A Love Letter

Ezra's profession as a scribe meant that he knew how to read and write. His lineage from the priestly line of Aaron meant that he was trained in the Law of Moses. His circumstances meant he was in Babylon, though Ezra longed to go to

Jerusalem. All of his life had been spent studying the precious words of God. Now his heart was set on studying God's holy Word in God's holy temple in Jerusalem. He longed to study and practice his true priestly calling, teaching others God's words and God's ways.

You don't need to be a priest or pastor to have a love for God's Word like Ezra. You just need to love the One who wrote it.

I once had a boyfriend who was a night security guard. He would occupy the early morning hours by writing love letters to me. When I would leave for work in the morning, I would find his letter under the windshield wiper of my car.

I would read those letters over and over and over again. Some of them were ten pages long. As a writer, I found it enchanting to have a guy write to me. At every possible moment—before work, during breaks or slow periods—I would read his letters to me. I would meditate on them and think about them even when I was occupied with daily tasks. I would search my memory for a phrase he used, then go back to refresh my memory on how he had worded it. I would ponder the nuances of meaning in different words and savor the flavor of each letter—some playful, others serious.

> God has written His love letter to us. We should long to read God's love letter over and over and over again.

I was not memorizing his letters in a mechanical way; I was allowing the words to saturate my mind so I could think about them even when I couldn't hold his letter in my hands.

In similar fashion, God has written His love letter to us. We should long to read God's love letter over and over and over again, at every possible moment, meditating on it throughout the day, pondering its meaning, and savoring the flavor.

What if my boyfriend gave me a ten-page letter and I was really busy, so I only read a paragraph and put it away? Then the next day I opened it and read one more paragraph. Then, out of a sense of duty, I did the same every day, except for the days I was too busy to take it out at all. How would that make my boyfriend feel? What would that say about my devotion and love for him?

If a relationship is reduced to duty, it's not much of a relationship. Duty says, "I have to"; devotion says, "I want to." Duty does only what is required; devotion seeks to do as much as possible. Duty borders on laziness; devotion borders on lavishness. Reading the Bible seems overwhelming when perceived as a duty, but when you love the Author, it is a joy to read it over and over and over again.

Duty may try to satisfy a perceived minimum requirement with a daily dose of God, but devotion tries to satisfy an unquenchable thirst for God and an addictive appetite for God's Word. Dr. Ron Frost encourages people to read the Bible at a brisk pace, though not on a particular schedule: "The purpose is to read the Bible for flow in the same way we might read any good book: whenever the time offers itself. That way we look at a free evening or Saturday morning as a 'chance' to read, not as a requirement, in order to meet the weekly increment."[2]

The size of the Bible might seem overwhelming to some people. However, it's about the same size as the latest novels, which many people cruise through in a matter of weeks. What if we approached the Bible with the same level of enthusiasm? It takes only eighteen hours to read the New Testament; many

2. R. N. Frost, *Discover the Power of the Bible: How God's Word Can Change Your Life* (Eugene, Ore.: Harvest House Publishers, 2000), 203.

people spend that much time in front of the television each week. It takes only seventy-two hours to read the entire Bible; many people spend that much time reading their favorite books and magazines. It's not just a matter of priorities; it's a matter of the heart.

Perhaps you've tried reading the Bible but found it difficult, either because of the language or because you are visually impaired, as I am. Let me provide a brief overview of some options that meet different needs.

People with limited exposure to the Bible or people who desire an easy-to-read Bible can choose from many contemporary versions that translate or paraphrase the text into familiar expressions: *Today's English Version,* the *New Living Translation,* the *Contemporary English Version,* the *English Standard Version,* the *Holman Christian Standard Bible,* and *The Message.*[3] In addition, the *New International Reader's Version* is written at a third-grade reading level, but it's not just for kids. If the Bible you're using seems too difficult or if you would like a refreshing change, try one of these. Reading them is a pleasure.

If you're ready for more than a casual reading of the Bible, several classic translations have stood the test of time: the *King James Version,* the *New King James Version,* the *New American Standard Bible,* and *The New International Version.* Both the *New American Standard Bible* and the *New International Version* are reliable and highly recommended for reading and in-depth study.[4]

3. One particularly fascinating version is *The Message,* by Eugene Peterson. It is both beautiful and, at times, shocking, which is the effect the Bible is meant to have in order to touch our hearts. One Bible translator has commented that if the Bible were being translated into English for the first time today, it would most resemble *The Message.*

4. Bibles can be purchased with or without study notes at the bottom of each page. While these notes can provide helpful information, I find that I spend my

With so many versions to choose from, you might want to compare several before making a decision. A good place to sample various Bible translations is www.BibleGateway.com. Reading God's love letter should be a pleasure rather than a chore, so choose a Bible that you can read with confidence and enthusiasm. If you are visually impaired, choose a large-print edition that is easy on the eyes. You will enjoy reading your Bible if the language is understandable and the printing is readable.

I highly recommend audio Bibles (cassette, CD, MP3). When I was reading large portions of Scripture in seminary, I discovered that I either got bogged down in the details and didn't keep a good pace, or I skimmed over it too quickly and didn't really absorb it. I began to put on an audio Bible and follow along in my own Bible. This kept me moving at a steady, comfortable pace.

Another advantage of an audio Bible is that when you are traveling or doing household chores, you can listen to the recording for extra exposure to the Word. Some people tell me that listening doesn't count (*Count for what?* I wonder), but I find that even if I am slightly distracted by other activities, God perks up my ears to hear the portions that speak to a particular need in my life. Also, we can gain much by rapid progression through the Bible, for we gain an understanding of the big picture and discover new connections between different portions of Scripture.

This goes back to the love letter frame of mind. Listening to God's words at every possible moment allows them to

---

time reading the notes instead of the Bible, so I prefer a Bible without notes. It's a matter of preference.

saturate our minds so we can think about them, even when we can't hold His letter in our hands.

Handling the Word of Truth

In addition to casually reading, we should carefully study God's love letter to us. Ezra "set his heart to study the law of the LORD" (Ezra 7:10). He determined to do more than read God's Word; he made it a priority to study God's Word.

Undoubtedly there are things you would like to know more about from the Bible. Somewhere in the back of your mind, you know the concepts that pique your curiosity and sense of wonder as you read the Bible. These are springboards for personal study. Don't put off Bible study because the word *study* reminds you of homework or cold pizza at 2 a.m. as you crammed for a history exam. Personal Bible study does not need to be complex or time consuming; it just requires taking an extra step for a few minutes.

If you don't know how to start studying the Bible, I recommend that you make two investments: buy a Bible dictionary and an exhaustive concordance. Many Bible resources are available electronically, so you may prefer to purchase a Bible software program or use online resources such as www. BibleGateway.com. Make sure you take the time to learn the resources you choose, however.

A Bible dictionary will allow you to look up people, places, things, and concepts to learn more about them. You might be amazed at how much additional insight you will gain by taking time to read a bit more information. When you read the Bible, you may find yourself wondering *who, where,* or *what is that?* That's when you need to follow your curiosity and pick up your Bible dictionary to find out. One step and a few minutes is all this form of additional study requires.

You should use a concordance that references the Bible translation you use most. For example, if you like to read from the *New International Version* (NIV), you will want an NIV concordance. Concordances are not just for finding a reference you forgot; they help you find the meaning of a word in the original Greek or Hebrew and help you locate every instance in the Bible where the original word was used, even if it is translated several ways in English.

Paul says, "Be diligent to present yourself approved to God as a workman who does not need to be ashamed, accurately handling the word of truth" (2 Timothy 2:15). When we do not accurately handle God's Word through careful study, we are left with nothing but to merely speculate about what it means. Sadly, too many group Bible studies consist of little more than each person responding to the question "What does this verse mean to you?" Bible interpretation is not a matter of opinion or speculation; it is a matter of "accurately handling the word of truth."

Doers of the Word

Not only should we be eager to immerse ourselves in God's love letter to us, we should be eager to do all that our Lover asks of us. Ezra understood this. He was committed to carrying out all that God revealed in His Word, for he "set his heart to study the law of the LORD and to practice it" (Ezra 7:10). Not only did he devote himself to obeying the law of God, but when he read it to the people in Jerusalem, they eagerly sought to obey it as well.

James warns believers to "prove yourselves doers of the word, and not merely hearers who delude themselves" (James 1:22). The people who heard Ezra read God's Word sought to obey it in its entirety, not selectively. They didn't pick and choose which parts to obey and which parts to disregard. They even signed a contract stating that they would obey it all. Whenever we selectively obey Scripture, we become hearers who delude ourselves, thinking that some parts of Scripture don't apply to us. To be deluded is to believe what is false, and to believe that portions of God's Word (the Old Testament, for example) are irrelevant is false.

God's Word—every word of it—was written to you and me. Sure, it contains historical accounts, but those accounts have meaning. They describe the character of God and how He lovingly, patiently deals with us. They also provide positive and negative examples of how people have interacted with God. These are lessons we can apply as we learn to interact with God.

Some people perceive the Bible as a big list of dos and don'ts. As our love relationship develops, we find our actions motivated by love. We should be passionately pursuing the things that will please our Lover.

When we love someone, we go out of our way to do things for that person, especially the things that we know please him or her. Simple things like putting the cap back on the toothpaste and picking up our shoes are not duties but little acts of devotion. In our relationship with God, simple things like forgiving others and being generous are not duties but little acts of devotion. We are not driven by duty, but by devotion. We eagerly put God's Word into action because we love Him.

The Living Word

In the New Testament, John testified, "the Word became flesh, and dwelt among us" (John 1:14). The Word of Life manifested itself in the life of Christ.

For this reason, the Word of God is not intended for academic consumption alone, although there is a need for careful study of it. Our relationship is not with the written Word, but with the Living Word, Christ Himself. As we become intimate with the Living Word, the written Word takes on new depths of meaning.

When you first met your spouse, your conversations were probably awkward as you tried to discern the intent behind this person's words. She offered to bring you coffee on the nights you work late, then she passed you a note with her phone number which read, "Call me if you want anything." Did she mean coffee, or a date?

As time went on, you learned to read each other. Often something will happen, and without a word, you will look at each other because you each know what the other is thinking. Other times you find yourselves finishing each other's sentences or simply reading each other's body language and facial expressions. In a multitude of ways, your relationship has given deeper meaning to your communication.

The same is true with God's Word. As we grow more intimate with God, His words become rich with meaning as we see more of His character in the text. The words have not changed, but our relationship has changed and brought new insight into the same old words we've read before.

For this reason, the Bible says, "The word of God is living and active and sharper than any two-edged sword, and piercing as far as the division of soul and spirit, of both joints and marrow, and able to judge the thoughts and intentions of the heart" (Hebrews 4:12). The Word is living and active. It is not the history of dead people, but the history of the living God.

The Word is living because it is one with God: "In the beginning was the Word and the Word was with God, and the Word was God" (John 1:1). The Word is active because it is sent forth from God to accomplish specific purposes:

> For as the rain and the snow come down from heaven,
> And do not return there without watering the earth
> And making it bear and sprout,
> And furnishing seed to the sower and bread to the
> eater;
> So will My word be which goes forth from My mouth;
> It will not return to Me empty,
> Without accomplishing what I desire,
> And without succeeding in the matter for which I sent
> it. (Isaiah 55:10–11)

The Living Word is a living being with specific purposes to accomplish. Therefore, our relationship with the Living Word should be anything but academic. Our relationship with the Word should be dynamic and interactive as we become more intimate.

God's Word Changes Us

Ezra provides an example of one who studied the lessons of God's Word and applied them to life. He led a great revival among his people as he read God's Word to them. When they heard God's Word, they were changed.

Have you ever noticed that if you hang around with someone who has a different accent that you begin to pick it up,
too? My mom's family is from Texas and Oklahoma. When
I'm around them, I start elongating my vowels and saying
"y'all." Days later I still find myself talking like them. Likewise, the more time we spend with God, through His Word,
the more we will pick up nearly imperceptible changes in the
way we think, act, and talk. Little by little, in ways we may
not notice at first, we become more like Him.

God's Word changes us by producing faith. Paul wrote,
"Faith comes from hearing, and hearing by the word of Christ"
(Romans 10:17). Faith is like a rubber band: As we stretch
it, it grows. The Word of God stretches us and challenges us
to be more than we were before.

God's Word changes us by causing growth. Peter used
this analogy: "Like newborn babies, long for the pure milk
of the word, so that by it you may grow in respect to salvation" (1 Peter 2:2). A baby doesn't really do anything to
cause its own growth except drink milk, something it loves
to do anyway. Likewise, we don't necessarily do anything
to cause our own growth except
thirst for God's Word, something
that should give us pleasure as it
nurtures us.

> As we engage in a lifelong dialogue with our Lover, we must learn to be good listeners.

God's Word changes us by equip-
ping us. Through His Word, God
gives us everything we need for our
spiritual growth: "All Scripture is
inspired by God and profitable for teaching, for reproof,
for correction, for training in righteousness; so that the man
of God may be adequate, equipped for every good work"
(2 Timothy 3:16–17).

As we interact with the Living Word in a vital and growing relationship, we cannot help but be changed. Eagerly reading and studying the divine love letter allow God's words to saturate our minds and spirits so that we can think about them even when we can't hold His letter in our hands—even when we are not having a formal quiet time. As we engage in a lifelong dialogue with our Lover, we must learn to be good listeners.

GOD'S WORD TO ME

1. What are the two parts of prayer, our dialogue with God?

   _____

   _____

   _____

   *Ezra: "Set His Heart to Study the Law of the Lord
   and to Practice It"*

2. What important things do we learn about Ezra in Ezra 7:6?

   _____

   _____

   _____

3. Why did Ezra come to Jerusalem (Ezra 7:10)?

   _____

   _____

   _____

   A Love Letter

4. Contrast *duty* and *devotion* in terms of our relationship with God.

   _____

   _____

   _____

5. Does it surprise you that it is possible to read the New Testament, and even the entire Bible, in so few hours? Compare with how many hours you spend reading novels, watching television, or using the Internet. Suggest a specific change you can make to free up time to spend in God's Word.

_____

_____

_____

_____

_____

6. What version of the Bible do you own? Do you enjoy reading this version? Why or why not? If you are finding it difficult to use the Bible you own, spend some time online at www.BibleGateway.com comparing some of the different Bible versions or go to a bookstore that sells Bibles and compare some of the versions it sells. Which version do you think would be most effective for your use? Why?

_____

_____

_____

_____

Handling the Word of Truth

7. What two investments are recommended as tools for Bible study? What does each do?

_____

_____

_____

Doers of the Word

8. What happens when we selectively obey Scripture, thinking that some parts of Scripture don't apply to us (James 1:22)?

_____

_____

_____

The Living Word

9. Who is the Living Word (John 1:1; John 1:14)?

_____

_____

10. How does your relationship with the Living Word help (or hinder, if that relationship isn't what it ought to be) your understanding of the Bible?

_____

_____

_____

God's Word Changes Us

11. What three ways does God's Word change us?

Romans 10:17 _____

1 Peter 2:2 _____

2 Timothy 3:16–17_____

12. How has God's Word changed you?

_____

_____

_____

Can You Hear Me Now?

At each stop during our nonstop day, God is saying to us, "Can you hear Me now?" Perhaps if He called our cell phone we would hear Him above the din of a dog, three kids, the television, computer games, and traffic. God doesn't want to be an item on our to-do lists; He wants to spend time with us while we do our to-do lists. He doesn't want to be an appointment in our Day Runner®; He wants to run with us to all our appointments.

Spending time with God is not something we do for a few minutes in the morning—maybe, if there's time. Spending time with God occurs all day. His Spirit lives within us, so by becoming aware of His presence we can carry on an ongoing conversation with Him.

Imagine that every two seconds God is saying to you, "Can you hear Me now?" How often are you responding? Your relationship with Him is the only wireless connection that is never broken. Just start responding like Samuel.

Samuel: "Speak, for Your Servant Is Listening"

"Samuel," whispered Hannah, her eyes brimming with tears. "You will always be my beloved son, the joy of my life."

She paused to clear her throat. "I have told you many times how I asked Yahweh for a son in this very place. I promised that if He gave me a son, I would give the boy back to the Lord. Yahweh heard my prayer and answered it: He gave me you, Samuel. You are no longer a babe; you are a boy, and I must fulfill my promise to give you to Yahweh."

> Spending time with God occurs all day. His Spirit lives within us, so by becoming aware of His presence we can carry on an ongoing conversation with Him.

Hannah continued, "Eli will watch after you like a father. He will teach you to serve the Lord. Obey him. I will visit you every year when we come to sacrifice. Be strong, Samuel, and courageous. Do not be afraid. Yahweh is with you, and you will be serving in His holy temple." Hannah kissed her son, and the boy began to cry. With her heart breaking into a million pieces, she held the boy but could not find her voice. No matter—the Lord knew her unuttered prayer, the desires of her heart, her anguish, love, and loyalty that made this moment so difficult. Yahweh knew.

Samuel, his face burning with tears, watched his father, Elkanah, take his wife by the arm to help her to her feet. In a moment that lasted a lifetime, Samuel watched Father put his arm around Mother and lead her away, her frame quivering with sobs. Samuel wanted to run after them, but he couldn't move.

When Eli put his hand on Samuel's shoulder, Samuel jumped as if suddenly awakened from a dream. "Come, my boy," the man spoke with kindness. Samuel turned to follow Eli, and then hesitated. He looked over his shoulder to see the figures of his parents in the distance. No, this was not a dream.

Although Samuel adapted quickly to his new home at the house of the Lord, he thought of his mother every night as he lay on his mat. He recalled her songs of praise and her prayers of thanksgiving. He often dreamed of his former days—of playing in the mud created when his mother tossed the dishwater, of running circles around their heifer, of chasing the chickens just to watch them scurry about, of Father calling him for supper: "Samuel!"

The boy was startled into wakefulness. For a moment, he was confused between two realities. He shook his head. No, the voice was so real that it must have been Eli calling for him.

"Here I am," called the boy, running to Eli.

The old man stirred from sleep. "Here I am," repeated Samuel, "for you called me."

"I did not call. Lie down again," Eli said, a bit gruffly.

Samuel shrugged and returned to his mat. *I guess it was just part of my dream.* He watched the steady flicker of the oil lamp, and before long, the boy drifted back into the shady reality of his dreams. This time he was polishing the gold lamp stand. On the other side of the curtain, he could hear Eli's sons brag in hushed voices about which one took the biggest portion of meat offered by those who came to sacrifice and about which of the women who served at the tent of the meeting they had seduced. When they heard the old man's shuffling steps, Eli's sons slithered under the flap of the tent. Eli called out, "Hophni! Phinehas!" No reply. "Samuel!"

The boy jolted as two realities again collided in the darkness. He ran to Eli. "Here I am, for you called me."

The old man rolled over to face the boy. With a bit of impatience he said, "I did not call, my son, lie down again."

Eli sighed as he tried to find a comfortable position on the hard floor.

Samuel shook his head in disbelief as he returned to his own mat on the floor. Eventually, the stillness overcame him as he slipped into slumber again.

"Samuel!"

The boy sat up. He could recall no dreams. This time he was certain. He approached Eli and said, "Here I am, for you called me."

Eli spoke tenderly this time. "Go lie down, and it shall be if He calls you that you shall say, 'Speak, Lord, for Your servant is listening.'"

Samuel returned to his mat. He could smell the oil from the lamp. *It must be close to dawn; the oil lamp is running low.* The boy felt as weary as if he had not slept at all, but Eli's instructions turned the gears of his mind. He strained to hear any sound. After a long vigil, the even purr of Eli's gentle snoring lulled the boy to sleep.

"Samuel! Samuel!"

The boy startled from sleep but was unafraid. "Speak, for Your servant is listening."

The Lord explained to the boy that He would soon judge the house of Eli because his sons brought a curse on themselves and Eli did not rebuke them.

Samuel lay down until morning, but this time sleep eluded him.

Things changed rapidly after that. The presence of the Lord returned to the house of the Lord.

Such news travels quickly, and the fervor of the people was palpable. Everywhere that the news spread, Samuel's name was spoken. The people called him a prophet, although the boy was too young to grasp the implications.

When the Philistines formed a battle line, Israel went out to fight but lost four thousand men in the battle. Eli's sons, Hophni and Phinehas, enamored with the power of God, took the ark of the covenant of God into the battlefield. Israel was again defeated, losing thirty thousand soldiers. Hophni and Phinehas were killed, and the Philistines captured the ark of God.

When Eli heard the news, he fell down and died. People who had been ecstatic over the news that the presence of the Lord had returned were now mourning, saying, "The glory has departed from Israel." However, the Philistines came under a curse from God, so they returned the ark. Israel allowed the ark to sit at Kiriath-jearim for twenty years.

During those twenty years, the boy, Samuel, became a man. He worked and ministered as a circuit judge, making annual trips to Bethel, Gilgal, Mizpah, and returning to his home in Ramah where he judged Israel all the days of his life.

For twenty years the ark of the Lord remained at Kiriath-jearim, and for twenty years the Philistines tormented Israel.

Then Samuel spoke.

The man who had been content to minister locally found himself compelled to speak to the nation. Now he understood what people once said when they referred to him as a prophet. As God's prophet, he must urge the people to repent, to remove their foreign gods, and give their hearts fully to the Lord alone. If they would repent, the Lord would deliver them from the hands of the Philistines.

They repented and gathered at Mizpah, where Samuel led them in a time of fasting, confession, and prayer. Samuel cried out to the Lord on their behalf, and God answered him.

The Philistines were subdued, and the hand of the Lord was against the Philistines all the days of Samuel.

When Samuel was old, he appointed his sons to succeed him as judges over Israel. However, his sons were dishonest judges, allowing money to turn their heads away from justice. So the elders of Israel approached Samuel and asked him to appoint a king to rule over them.

No doubt, Samuel recalled his youth, when Eli grew old and lost touch with the Lord and lost control of his sons. Samuel's first encounter with the Lord had been concerning God's judgment of Eli and his sons. Had Samuel's situation become so similar—an old man, out-of-touch and out-of-control—that God was prepared to reject and remove him, too?

Samuel prayed to the Lord.

God answered Samuel: "They have not rejected you, but they have rejected Me from being king over them."

So Samuel instructed and warned the people about what life under a king would entail. When they still insisted on having a king, God instructed Samuel to anoint Saul as king.

Samuel assembled the people of Israel and publicly demonstrated, by the casting of lots, that God had chosen Saul to be king over them. As Samuel addressed the people, he called to the Lord, and the Lord sent thunder and rain during the dry harvest season.

Therefore, all the people greatly feared the Lord and Samuel. "Pray for us so that we may not die," they said.

"Do not fear," Samuel assured them. "The Lord will not abandon His people. Serve Him with all your heart. As for me, far be it from me that I should sin against the Lord by ceasing to pray for you."

My Opening Monologue

For Samuel, prayer was not a speech or soliloquy; prayer was a meaningful dialogue with God. When God spoke, Samuel listened; and when Samuel spoke, God listened. Throughout Samuel's life and ministry, there was always two-way conversation with God.

As a new believer, I used to bristle at the concept of prayer. What was the point of telling a sovereign God the things that He already knew? Prayer was a meaningless monologue to me. My prayer life was transformed once it moved from monologue to dialogue.

This transformation occurred as I learned to bring my problems to God, searching my heart and God's Word for biblical truths that would give me clear guidance on specific matters. Instead of giving God a daily speech, I began to converse with Him, seeking His advice and wisdom in every situation. As far as I'm concerned, I quit my quiet time and these meaningless monologues and began having ongoing, spontaneous conversations with God.

> I quit my quiet time and these meaningless monologues and began having ongoing, spontaneous conversations with God.

The key to moving from monologue to dialogue is listening, as a habit, throughout the day. Jan Johnson likewise believes that listening should be integrated into our daily activities as we converse with God throughout the day: "Listening to God is part of our continual conversation with Him. It is not limited to a portion of our quiet time set aside for listening."[1]

1. Johnson, *Enjoying the Presence of God*, 92.

Reduce the Noise

In the stillness of the pre-dawn hours, Samuel heard from God for the first time. Silence is a beautiful thing, a rare commodity in modern society. If silence were an animal, it would be an endangered species. It seems like everything about our culture produces noise: radio, television, and household appliances, just for starters. Even if we took care of the noise within our control, there would still be the racket made by neighbors in the adjoining apartments, the drone of local traffic, the banging of construction, the high-pitched whine of lawnmowers, and the periodic accent of trains, planes, and emergency vehicles.

It is not enough to reduce external noise; we must also reduce internal noise and mental clutter that occupy our minds. It is not something we can turn off like a switch. Instead, it is more like cleaning house.

Some people are afraid of silence. That's why one of the strictest punishments in our penal system is solitary confinement. Many people cannot bear to be alone with their thoughts, so they maintain an environment of noise to distract themselves. Jan Johnson observes, "Frenzy fills our lives because if we stop running, we may have to face an empty silence or a nagging voice from God." She also notes why some people avoid solitude: "In solitude, our character defects come to the surface."[2]

Robert Mulholland explains the interrelationship among silence, solitude, and prayer: "Prayer is the outgrowth of both silence and solitude. In silence we let go of our manipulative control. In solitude we face up to what we are in

2. Johnson, *Enjoying the Presence of God,* 119, 127.

the depths of our being. Prayer then becomes the offering of who we are to God: the giving of that broken, unclean, grasping, manipulative self to God for the work of God's grace in our lives."[3]

To enjoy long periods of silence, one must be very comfortable with who he or she is as a person. If negative self-talk, guilt, fear, remorse, or loneliness occupies a person's mental activity, silence might seem unbearable. However, those are exactly the points at which we can open a dialogue with God, telling Him our troubling thoughts and seeking His comfort, help, and healing. Johnson agrees that these disturbing thoughts serve as indicators to seek God: "Any time we sense an anxious emptiness inside, this becomes a signal to spend time with God and listen for His still, small voice."[4] As we become more secure with who we are and who God is, we find that positive (or at least neutral) thoughts occupy our mental activity in the silent periods.

I'm not talking about five minutes of silence scheduled into a quiet time; I'm talking about developing a quiet heart. Although there are things we can do to create a quiet environment, much of the external noise is beyond our control, but when we learn to be quiet within ourselves, we can enjoy peace within our hearts and minds anywhere.

> It is there, within the quiet sanctuary of our hearts, that we can enjoy God's presence regardless of our environment or activities.

Inner serenity can become a state of being to which we long to return at every possible moment. It is there, within the quiet sanctuary of our hearts, that we

---

3. Mulholland, *Invitation to a Journey,* 140.
4. Johnson, *Enjoying the Presence of God,* 128.

can enjoy God's presence regardless of our environment or activities. Mother Teresa explains:

> But to be able to pray we need silence
>   silence of the heart.
> The soul needs time to go away and pray . . .
> And if we don't have that silence then we don't know
>   how to pray.[5]

At times we will still need to slip away to a place of environmental silence and solitude, just as Jesus slipped away to pray. There we can listen to our hearts for any garbage or mental clutter that comes to the surface. If we deal with mental clutter on a regular basis, we can maintain the quiet sanctuary of our hearts and take that tranquility with us back into our hectic lives. There is such a thing as peace in the midst of a storm.

Peace and Quiet

We can learn to be quiet within ourselves by praying about each bit of mental clutter until we find peace. That's what Samuel did. When he feared that the people had rejected him by asking for a king and that God was about to reject and remove him just as He had removed Eli, Samuel brought these fears to the Lord.

Anything that disturbs our sense of inner peace is not of God, so we can follow God by pursuing the course of action that leads to peace. For instance, if I have to make a decision, I contemplate which option gives me a sense of peace and

5. Mother Teresa, *Words to Love by . . .* , 42.

which arouses anxiety. I pursue the option that leads to peace. Listening to God can be as simple as listening to what our hearts and bodies are telling us. It's not that God speaks the answer, but God's answer is clear if we listen to our hearts.

People occasionally wonder why God does not speak to us directly like He did on certain occasions in the Bible. Although we might prefer the dramatic or wish that God would make certain things absolutely clear by speaking them aloud or writing on a billboard for us, God still speaks.

God created us as spiritual beings, capable of relating to Him as Spirit. The Holy Spirit is the vital link between the human mind and the mind of God. The Spirit of God knows the thoughts of God (1 Corinthians 2:11), and the Spirit abiding in us conveys those thoughts to us in a way we can understand. Jesus explained this to His disciples, saying, "But when He, the Spirit of truth, comes, He will guide you into all the truth; for He will not speak on His own initiative, but whatever He hears, He will speak; and He will disclose to you what is to come" (John 16:13). God made us spiritual beings for the express purpose of facilitating communication with a Spirit God. Again, I would emphasize that this generally occurs in very natural ways, such as God giving us peace about a particular decision or bringing to mind a Scripture verse that helps us.

Jesus said, "the Helper, the Holy Spirit, whom the Father will send in My name, He will teach you all things, and bring to your remembrance all that I said to you" (John 14:26). As we discussed in the previous chapter, God communicates to us through His written Word. The Holy Spirit brings the Word of God to mind at appropriate times to guide us in the way of truth. This highlights the importance of spending time in the Word of God, because He cannot bring to mind what was never in our mind.

Hearing Voices?

In the previous chapter I made the point that God's Spirit communicates to us *primarily* through His written Word. I did not say that He communicates to us *only* through His written Word, as some people believe.[6]

In case you are feeling uncomfortable with the notion that we are privy to the words of God apart from the written Word, let me assure you that this typically occurs in a natural way. For instance, all humans have a conscience. For unbelievers, conscience is shaped mostly by social norms and upbringing, but the Holy Spirit has direct access to the consciences of believers. Believers may feel the nudge of God moving them away from one thing or toward another. Sometimes what we may call intuition is really a nudge of the Spirit in the life of a believer. Likewise, the direction of the Spirit may be as subtle as a personal preference, leaving us entirely unaware that the preference originated from God.

People often refer to "the still, small voice" of God. It's not an audible voice, but it is no less distinct. Some believers are uncomfortable with this notion, and perhaps justifiably so, because there is room for subjectivity (hearing what you want to hear) or even opening oneself up to the voice of Satan's minions. Nonetheless, Jesus seemed to indicate that we should

6. Some believers object to the notion that we are privy to the words of God apart from the written Word. For them, the Bible is the only voice of God, as it were. Dallas Willard speaks to this line of thinking: "Today something that could aptly be called 'Bible deism' is prevalent, particularly in conservative religious circles. Classical deism, associated with the extreme rationalism of the sixteenth to eighteenth centuries, held that God created his world complete and perfect and then went away, leaving us to make what we could of it, with no individualized communication either through the Bible or otherwise." (Dallas Willard, *Hearing God: Developing a Conversational Relationship with God,* 3rd ed. [Downers Grove, Ill.: InterVarsity Press, 1999]), 107.

be able to hear and recognize the words of God: "He who is of God hears the words of God; for this reason you do not hear them, because you are not of God" (John 8:47).

So if Jesus indicated that we should be able to hear God's voice, why do so many believers not hear His voice? Dallas Willard offers this explanation: "Perhaps we do not hear the voice [of God] because we do not expect to hear it. Then again, perhaps we do not expect it because we know that we fully intend to run our lives on our own and have never seriously considered anything else. The voice of God would therefore be an unwelcome intrusion into our plans."[7] We can either run our lives with God as our co-pilot or surrender control to God. Only then are we in a position to hear what God has to say. Only then will we be still and listen.

The Voice of Experience

Though he was a priest at God's temple, Eli had not heard from God in years. Was it that God was no longer speaking to him, or that Eli simply could not recognize His voice? Samuel had to awaken Eli several times before the priest realized that it was God who was calling out to the young boy.

Samuel *learned* to recognize God's voice. He didn't get it right on the first try or the second or the third. Hearing God's voice and responding appropriately come with experience.

Jan Johnson admits there is a learning curve associated with recognizing God's voice: "By practicing the presence of God, we learn to recognize His voice and stop confusing it with our own."[8] This brings me back to the objection some raise that

7. Willard, *Hearing God*, 71.
8. Johnson, *Enjoying the Presence of God*, 93.

listening for a still, small voice is subject to our own wishes, or worse, that we might begin to hear the words of a counterfeit god. This is a valid concern. John warned believers, "Beloved, do not believe every spirit, but test the spirits to see whether they are from God . . . By this you know the Spirit of God: every spirit that confesses that Jesus Christ has come in the flesh is from God" (1 John 4:1–2). Anything that is contrary to the written Word of God cannot be the word of the Holy Spirit. Discernment is learned through experience. Hebrews 5:14 says, "Solid food is for the mature, who because of practice have their senses trained to discern good and evil."

> The better you know God, the easier it is to recognize His voice.

This ability to learn discernment is a very simple process: If my sister called me, I would recognize her voice instantly because I know her so well. If a recent acquaintance called, it would take more than a "hello" for me to discern the identity of the voice. Even with some extended conversation I may not be able to recognize the voice. When you know someone, you recognize his or her voice. The same is true with God. The better you know God, the easier it is to recognize His voice.

CAN YOU HEAR ME NOW?

1. Imagine that every two seconds God is saying to you, "Can you hear Me now?" How often are you responding?

   _____

   _____

   _____

   Samuel: "Speak, for Your Servant Is Listening"

2. How many times did it take Samuel to respond to God's voice (1 Samuel 3:1–10)?

   _____

   _____

   _____

3. How does the Bible depict Samuel's prayer life (1 Samuel 7:9; 8:6–7)?

   _____

   _____

   _____

   My Opening Monologue

4. When you talk to God, does it seem like a meaningless monologue or a dynamic dialogue?

   _____

   _____

Reduce the Noise

5. Do you enjoy silence or avoid it? Why?

_____

_____

_____

6. When you are alone with your thoughts, what do you hear? Troubling thoughts such as negative self-talk, guilt, fear, anxiety, remorse, or loneliness become points at which we can open a dialogue with God. What are the benefits of telling God your troubling thoughts?

_____

_____

_____

_____

7. List three ways you can reduce the external noise and distractions—even for brief periods—so you can begin to listen to your thoughts and deal with them. (For example, turn off the radio in the car.)
   1. _____
   2. _____
   3. _____

Peace and Quiet

8. What does the Bible teach about the Holy Spirit as the vital link between the human mind and the mind of God (1 Corinthians 2:11; John 16:13)?

_____

_____

_____

9. Why is it important to spend time in God's Word? What is the Holy Spirit's role in this regard (John 14:26)?

_____

_____

_____

Hearing Voices?

10. Christians disagree on whether the Bible is the only voice of God or whether God communicates to us in individualized ways. Conscience, intuition, and personal preference may be subtle ways God communicates to us. What did Jesus say about this (John 8:47)?

_____

_____

_____

11. What was Dallas Willard's explanation for why people do not hear the voice of God? Do you agree or disagree? Why?

_____

_____

_____

The Voice of Experience

12. How will you know if you are hearing from God or if you are hearing what you want to hear (1 John 4:1–2; Hebrews 5:14)?

_____

_____

_____

The Ultimate Reality Show

*T*hings happen in real life that you couldn't make up if you tried. Real life can be stranger than fiction. That's a simple truth that television producers realized a few years ago when they began to create reality shows like *Survivor* and *Amazing Race*. Willing participants are subjected to a variety of settings and experiences. They face physical and psychological challenges, such as overcoming fear, racing against time, or interpersonal friction, to observe how they really behave under extreme pressure.

We each live the ultimate reality show, enduring our own set of physical and psychological challenges, and God is watching. He's not a mere spectator, though, but a participant on our team. However, there's no hiding the realities of our lives from Him. He knows it all.

Jeremiah experienced the ultimate reality show in his lifetime. He relentlessly cried out to God until he became known as the weeping prophet.

Jeremiah: "Ah, Lord God"

"I knew you, Jeremiah, before I even formed you in the womb. Before you were born, I had a special purpose for your life: I have appointed you as a prophet," said the Lord.

"But I do not know how to speak," gasped Jeremiah.

"You will speak all that I command you," assured the Lord. Then the Lord reached out and touched Jeremiah's mouth and said, "I have put My words in your mouth. Declare in Judah that I am bringing evil from the north to destroy your cities, even Jerusalem."

Jeremiah cried out, "Ah, Lord God! You have deceived us, saying 'You will have peace,' but a sword is at our throat. Oh my soul! I am in such anguish that my heart is about to pound out of my chest."

"Search the streets of Jerusalem, Jeremiah. If you can find a man—just one—who does justice and seeks truth, I will pardon Jerusalem," said the Lord.

Jeremiah searched, but the poor were ignorant and did not know the ordinance of God, and the great, although they knew the ordinance of God, had turned away from the way of the Lord.

Then Jeremiah prayed, "My heart is weak with sorrow. I mourn for the brokenness of my people. Is there no physician who can restore the health of my people? Where is the wise man that can understand these things?"

The Lord replied, "Do not let a wise man boast of his wisdom, but let him who boasts boast that he understands and knows Me. Now stand at the temple gate and declare My message, even though they will not listen."

The men of Anathoth, Jeremiah's hometown, threatened to kill him if he did not quit speaking in the name of the Lord. So Jeremiah prayed, "Lord who judges righteously, I have committed my cause to You."

The Lord replied, "I am about to bring disaster on the men of Anathoth, but be warned: Even your father and brothers have dealt treacherously with you. They may say nice things to you, but do not believe them."

Again Jeremiah sought the Lord, "Why, Lord? Why do the wicked prosper, and how long is this going to last?"

"I am allowing wicked nations to uproot my people and take them into captivity, but I will again have compassion on them and will bring them back," said the Lord.

"Ah, Lord God!" exclaimed Jeremiah. "The other prophets are telling the people not to worry because there will be no war or famine."

"They are prophesying falsely in My name," said the Lord. "I have not spoken to them. Those who claim there will be no sword or famine will die by the sword or famine."

In despair, Jeremiah prayed, "Lord, for Your sake I endure the reproach of my persecutors. Don't forget about me, for I have been called by Your name and because of Your hand upon me, I sat alone. Are You reliable or not?"

The Lord rebuked Jeremiah, "If you repent and return to Me, I will restore you. Sift the good from the worthless attitudes and have faith that your personal enemies will not prevail. I will deliver you from their violent ways. For cursed is the one whose heart turns away from the Lord, but blessed is the one who trusts in the Lord."

With this, Jeremiah reaffirmed his commitment to God: "Heal me, Lord. Save me. You know that I have spoken Your words, even when others harassed me. You are my refuge. Let my persecutors be put to shame, but do not shame me before them."

Meanwhile, Jeremiah's enemies continued to conspire against him, saying, "Let's make plans against Jeremiah. Let's verbally attack him and discredit his words."

Again Jeremiah prayed, "Listen to what my opponents are saying! Remember how I interceded on their behalf, that you would turn away your wrath from Judah? You know all their deadly plans against me, so deal with them accordingly."

Jeremiah went to the temple courtyard and proclaimed, "The Lord says, 'I am about to destroy this city because they have not listened to My words.'"

When Pashhur, the priest, heard this, he had Jeremiah beaten and put in stocks near the house of the Lord. The next day he released Jeremiah.

Jeremiah prayed, "I have become a laughingstock all day long. Everyone mocks me when I proclaim Your words. Yet if I say, 'I will not speak for God anymore,' my heart burns within me. My trusted friends watch for my downfall, but You are like a champion prizefighter in my corner of the arena. Thank you for delivering me from evildoers. Still, I wonder why I was even born. Why was I born to endure trouble, sorrow, and shame all my life?"

On another occasion, Jeremiah was speaking in the house of the Lord, and when he finished speaking, the prophets, priests, and people grabbed him and said, "You must die." They drug him before the city officials and asked for a death sentence under the charge of treason. In his defense Jeremiah said, "The Lord sent me to prophesy against this house and against this city. Do whatever you wish to me, but if you put me to death, you will bring innocent blood on yourselves. I am in your hands."

Then the city officials told the prophets and priests, "No death sentence. This man has spoken on behalf of God to us."

So Jeremiah was not given over to the people who wanted to put him to death.

During the reign of Jehoiakim, the Lord said to Jeremiah, "Write on a scroll all the words I have written to you from the days of Josiah until now. Perhaps if the people hear of the calamity to come, they will repent, and I will forgive them."

So Jeremiah dictated to Baruch, the scribe, all the words that the Lord had spoken to him. Then Jeremiah told Baruch, "I have been banned from the temple, and so you must go read from the scroll in the Lord's house. Perhaps the people will turn from their evil ways."

Baruch read from the book in the presence of the people. When one of the scribes heard it, he reported it to the king's house. King Jehoiakim asked Baruch to bring the scroll and read it to him. After the king listened to three or four columns, he said, "Why have you written that the king of Babylon will destroy this land?" Then Jehoiakim cut the scroll with a knife and threw it into the fire, and the scroll was completely destroyed.

After Nebuchadnezzar, king of Babylon, made Zedekiah the king of Judah, Zedekiah sent his priests to Jeremiah. They delivered the king's message to him: "Please inquire of the Lord for us. Will the Lord be merciful so that the enemy withdraws from us?"

Jeremiah replied, "Tell King Zedekiah that the Lord says, 'I will personally make war against you. Pharaoh's army will return to Egypt, and the Babylonians will resume the siege until they capture and destroy the city.'"

During the siege, Zedekiah imprisoned Jeremiah for treason because the prophet was proclaiming that God would give the city over to Babylon. This happened when Jeremiah left the city to conduct some business in the land of Benjamin. As he left the Benjamin Gate, the captain of the guard arrested Jeremiah, accusing him of going over to the Babylonians. The king's officials beat Jeremiah and imprisoned him in the dungeon.

After many days, King Zedekiah sent for Jeremiah to meet him secretly in the house of the Lord. The king said, "Is there a word from the Lord? Tell me the truth and do not hold back."

Jeremiah retorted, "If I tell you, you will put me to death."

But the king swore, "I will not put you to death or hand you over to the men who seek your life."

So Jeremiah said, "Surrender to the Babylonians and you will live."

Zedekiah admonished Jeremiah, "For the sake of your life, do not mention this conversation to anyone. If anyone asks you, tell them you were petitioning the king not to make you return to the dungeon to die there." Then King Zedekiah ordered that Jeremiah be relocated to the court of the guard-house and that he be given a loaf of bread daily, so long as bread was available.

Jeremiah continued to proclaim the word of the Lord to passers by. The officials again raised the charge of treason against him, so the king allowed them to do as they wished. Then the men threw Jeremiah into a cistern with no water in it, and he sank into the mud.

An Ethiopian in the king's palace heard of it and told the king that the officials had thrown Jeremiah into a cistern to starve to death. The king told him, "Rescue Jeremiah before he dies." So the Ethiopian took thirty men, and they lowered ropes and worn-out clothes down to Jeremiah.

"Put these rags around the ropes under your arms," they said. Then they pulled him out of the cistern.

When the Babylonians breached the city wall in 586 BC, Nebuchadnezzar ordered his captain of the bodyguard to find and rescue Jeremiah so that no harm would come to him, for the Babylonians had heard of his messages from God favoring their nation. They found Jeremiah in the court of the guardhouse and released him. The captain of the bodyguard said, "I am freeing you today. If you wish to come with me to Babylon, I will look after you; if not, you are free to go wherever you wish."

Although most of the population had been deported to Babylon, Jeremiah stayed among the people left in the land. The people asked Jeremiah to pray that God would tell them what to do, promising to obey whatever the Lord commanded. Jeremiah told them, "The Lord says, 'Stay in this land and I will relent of the calamity I have inflicted upon you. If you do not stay, but flee to Egypt, the sword and famine will follow you and you will die there.'"

The people responded in anger, "You are lying. The Lord did not say that." So they did not obey the Lord. One of the military leaders forced the people, including Jeremiah and Baruch, to go to Egypt, against the Lord's command. Yet even in Egypt, Jeremiah continued to proclaim the word of the Lord. He declared that Israel would be restored and pardoned and that Babylon would eventually be judged for sins against Judah.

Shared Experiences

"Prayer is a meaningless monologue, telling God what He already knows," I used to tell my friend, who was attending

Bible college. The two of us had some vigorous discussions on the subject as I went through a frustrating phase where prayer seemed pointless. However, my friend wasn't getting through to me any better than I was getting through to God.

Although it was exasperating at the time, the questions raised during that phase eventually transformed my thinking about how to relate to God. The difference in how we relate to God is in how we perceive God. If we perceive God as distant, we communicate as if we are placing a call to an out-of-town friend, describing the details of what's going on in our life. If we perceive God as present, we can talk to Him as if He were the friend who was there when it happened, so we can skip the details and get to the heart of the matter.

> If we perceive God as present, we can talk to Him as if He were the friend who was there when it happened, so we can skip the details and get to the heart of the matter.

I thought that if God already knew the details, there was nothing left to talk about. Wrong. When you share experiences with a friend, it does not mean that you have nothing to talk about; shared experiences mean that you can talk about the significance of life's events.

When my brother and I went to our first doubleheader at a major league baseball stadium, we cheered our team through two come-from-behind victories. After the games, we were non-stop chatter. We had shared the same experience; we both knew the events that had transpired. The shared experience meant we could skip discussing the details and talk about how the events made us feel—the exhilaration of going from certain defeat to an unlikely victory, twice in the same day.

Shared experiences open the door for deeper communication, and these shared experiences become the building blocks for a more intimate relationship. For Jeremiah, prayer was anything but a meaningless monologue. His communication with God was a constant dialogue in which he would even interrupt God. Whether he was in the temple, the king's house, or prison, Jeremiah was real with God. Intimacy with God comes from reality with God in a variety of settings. If reality with God leads to intimacy with God, why is it so difficult to be "real" with God?

Hide and Seek

Like Adam and Eve who tried to hide from God after they sinned, we often try to hide, but God asked Jeremiah, "Can a man hide himself in hiding places so I do not see him?" (Jeremiah 23:24). Obviously not.

We find it amusing that an ostrich will stick its head in a hole and think that it is hiding. Yet we essentially do the same thing when we try to hide from God. And don't try to convince yourself that you don't try to hide; we all do it in one form or another. When we talk to God about our superficial needs (health, finances, and external needs) but do not bring to Him our needy, broken, manipulative, prideful hearts, we are sticking our heads in the sand. We think that if we ignore the truth about the condition of our hearts, God won't notice. Maybe we've kept our heads in a hole so long that we have too much sand between the ears!

Jeremiah tried to put his head in the sand. He tried to stop speaking for God, but his heart burned within him (Jeremiah 20:9). There's a word for that: denial. Jeremiah tried to deny who God made him to be. He tried to deny his true calling, the special purpose for which God had made him, but putting his head in the sand gave Jeremiah spiritual heartburn.

In the previous chapter, we discussed how silence and solitude could reveal the noise of disturbing thoughts and attitudes of the heart. Rather than pushing them aside with constant activity and a multitude of defense mechanisms, these thoughts can become springboards for communication with God. In this manner, "We are taking every thought captive to the obedience of Christ" (2 Corinthians 10:5). By taking every thought and emotion to Him—the good, the bad, and the ugly—we are developing intimacy with God through reality with God. When our lives are transparent and essentially naked before God, we have accepted reality. By sharing those things with God and openly discussing the unvarnished truth about the condition of our heart, intimacy results.

> By taking every thought and emotion to Him—the good, the bad, and the ugly—we are developing intimacy with God through reality with God.

When we watch God peel back the defense mechanisms in our lives and expose the ugly rottenness lurking in the shadows, we get to play a new game: truth or dare.

Truth or Dare

There are very few people who are genuine risk takers. We are taught to play it safe, but life, especially life with God at its center, seems like a giant game of truth or dare. Are we willing to be truthful about who we are? Do we dare to trust

God with our lives? Are we willing to embrace life as the great adventure and live on the edge? Taking risks is an opportunity to experience a thrill like never before, but many people back away and watch others accept the challenge. It's risky to expose our sinful hearts to God because He will likely pull out His knife for heart surgery. However, the one who is willing to be gut-level honest with God is going to experience the joys of intimacy with God. Those who prefer to play it safe will sit back and watch others experience intimacy with God.

Jeremiah had taken risks for God. He spoke for God and was persecuted for it. He reached a point where he wasn't sure he wanted to keep playing truth or dare. He was on the receiving end of so much persecution that he wondered if God was deceiving him. So rather than hiding his true feelings, Jeremiah took them to God: "Why has my pain been perpetual and my wound incurable, refusing to be healed? Will You indeed be to me like a deceptive stream with water that is unreliable?" (Jeremiah 15:18). Jeremiah wanted to know if God was reliable: Could he dare to trust God with his life?

> God dares each of us to trust Him. He firmly presses us to trust Him a bit more than we did before.

God's response? Truth or dare. He told Jeremiah to tell the truth about his worthless attitudes and dare to trust God with his life, even when faced with persecution. The Lord went on to say, "Cursed is the man . . . whose heart turns away from the LORD . . . Blessed is the man who trusts in the LORD and whose trust is the LORD" (Jeremiah 17:5, 7).

God dares each of us to trust Him. He firmly presses us to trust Him a bit more than we did before. Some of us will back away and watch others take the challenge. Gradually, such hearts will turn away from the Lord. Some of us will accept the challenge and experience the thrill of jumping into God's arms, trusting that He will catch us. These are the ones who will experience the joys of intimacy with God.

It Hurts So Good

Jeremiah was miserable speaking for God and enduring the consequences. He tried to stop speaking for God, but his heart burned within him, so he accepted his calling, embraced his pain, and brought it to God. By embracing his pain, he was able to be real with God. No more hiding. No more head in the sand.

If you've ever been on the receiving end of a back massage, you know that it feels so good, until those strong hands find a sore spot. As they begin to knead a muscle that feels like it is tied up in a knot, you may find yourself alternately saying, "Oh, it hurts. Don't stop. Oh, it hurts. Don't stop." That's because it hurts so good.

When we allow ourselves to be real with God, when we accept the risk of playing truth or dare with Him, God will find the sore spots in our lives. Then we experience the same phenomenon: It hurts so good.

Sometimes when I pray for others, I ask God to put His finger on their point of pain so that healing can come. In other words, *make them miserable, Lord, so they will seek You.* (You might want to think twice about asking me to pray for you.)

Recently, I had the courage to actually pray that for myself: *Lord, put Your finger on my point of pain so that healing can come.* Almost immediately, I felt the deep ache in my heart as God revealed my feelings of inferiority in a certain area. It hurt.

I immediately recognized it as the source of some behavioral problems I was experiencing, yet my defense mechanisms had been hiding the truth. This was one of those rare moments when I was stripped of my defense mechanisms and forced to be totally honest with God and myself about the ugly truth. It was painful and emotionally disturbing, but God's presence gave me the strength to face it. I simultaneously felt incredibly vulnerable and incredibly safe.

We can simultaneously feel extremely vulnerable and extremely safe with God. When the truth is exposed, we feel vulnerable and defenseless, but we can also know that God is not trying to hurt us but to heal us. In that respect, it hurts so good.

If we are willing to play truth or dare with God, then we can skip the timid prayers, as if we thought we were bothering God with our meager requests. If we are bold enough to be real with God to the point that it hurts so good, then we can be bold enough to ask God to help us: "Therefore let us draw near with confidence to the throne of grace, so that we may receive mercy and find grace to help in time of need" (Hebrews 4:16). When we allow God to expose our point of need, we can run into the throne room of God, draw close to Him, and ask Him to gently heal our wounds. Like Jeremiah, we can cry out to God: "Heal me, O LORD, and I will be healed; save me and I will be saved, for You are my praise" (Jeremiah 17:14).

Bragging Rights

In the ultimate reality show of our lives, we face many difficult circumstances that push us beyond our limits. At times we may feel unsure of how to proceed. We may encounter physical or emotional afflictions. We may be treated unfairly or even persecuted. Jeremiah was so depressed by his adversity that he wished he had not been born, but he encouraged himself by focusing on God rather than on his problems: "The LORD is with me like a dread champion; therefore my persecutors will stumble and not prevail" (Jeremiah 20:11). We may not feel like a "survivor," and we may want to drop out of our own "amazing race," but God is our partner through it all. We have a Champion in our corner.

Life is difficult so that we will rely on God: "We have this treasure in earthen vessels, so that the surpassing greatness of the power will be of God and not from ourselves" (2 Corinthians 4:7). We are fragile vessels, but God's resurrection power is available to work in and through our lives. If God can raise the dead, He can certainly handle anything we encounter in life. Jeremiah cried out to God: "Ah Lord GOD! Behold, You have made the heavens and the earth by Your great power and by Your outstretched arm! Nothing is too difficult for You" (Jeremiah 32:17). When life seems difficult, we can remind ourselves that nothing is too difficult for God.

When we rely on God, we cannot take credit for ourselves; we can only boast about what God has done. What do we have to brag about, anyway? We are humble suppliants, mere beggars, seeking help from a Champion. Paul accepted his weaknesses as opportunities to receive God's power: "Most gladly, therefore, I will rather boast about my weaknesses, so that the power of Christ may dwell in me. Therefore I am well content with weaknesses, with insults, with distresses, with persecutions, with difficulties, for Christ's sake; for when I am weak, then I am strong" (2 Corinthians 12:9–10). By admitting our weaknesses and letting God put His finger on our point of pain, we can receive God's strength and healing.

God told Jeremiah, "Let not a wise man boast of his wisdom, and let not the mighty man boast of his might, let not a rich man boast of his riches; but let him who boasts boast of this, that he understands and knows Me, that I am the LORD who exercises loving-kindness, justice and righteousness on earth; for I delight in these things" (Jeremiah 9:23–24). We can only boast that we know God. Many people know *about* God, but intimacy is about knowing someone at the deepest levels. When we are willing to get real with God, intimacy will develop. We won't just know that God delights in love, justice, and righteousness; we will experience those qualities of God as we partner with Him through our ultimate reality show.

> When we are willing to get real with God, intimacy will develop.

THE ULTIMATE REALITY SHOW

1. We each live the ultimate reality show. What life challenges are you facing in your reality show?

   _____

   _____

   _____

Jeremiah: "Ah, Lord God"

2. Jeremiah tried to deny who God made him to be. He tried to deny his true calling, the special purpose for which God had made him. What happened when Jeremiah tried to stop speaking for God (Jeremiah 20:9)?

   _____

   _____

   _____

   _____

Shared Experiences

3. Intimacy with God comes from reality with God in a variety of settings. If reality with God leads to intimacy with God, why is it so difficult to be "real" with God?

   _____

   _____

   _____

   _____

Hide and Seek

4. When we talk to God about our superficial needs but do not bring to Him our needy, broken, manipulative, prideful hearts, we are sticking our heads in the sand. We think that if we ignore the truth about the condition of our hearts that God won't notice. In what ways, or what parts of your life, are you trying to hide from God?

_____

_____

_____

5. By taking every thought and emotion to God—the good, the bad, and the ugly—we are developing intimacy with God through reality with God. Take time to discuss with God the unvarnished truth about the condition of your heart. What do you think will be some of the benefits of "getting real" with Him?

_____

_____

_____

Truth or Dare

6. The one who is willing to be gut-level honest with God is going to experience the joys of intimacy with God. Those who prefer to play it safe will sit back and watch others experience intimacy with God. Which one describes you? Which one do you want to be? If change is necessary, what will you do differently?

_____

_____

_____

7. Some of us will back away from the Lord and watch others take the challenge. Some of us will accept the challenge and experience the thrill of jumping into God's arms, trusting that He will catch us. What does God say about these two types of people (Jeremiah 17:5, 7)?

_____

_____

_____

_____

It Hurts So Good

8. It's a risky prayer: *Lord, put Your finger on my point of pain so that healing can come.* Are you bold enough to pray that honestly? Why? What might happen if you do?

_____

_____

_____

_____

9. If we are bold enough to be vulnerable with God, what promise do we have (Hebrews 4:16)?

_____

_____

_____

Bragging Rights

10. Life is difficult so that we will rely on God. Jeremiah encouraged himself by focusing on God rather than on his problems. What are some of the encouraging

thoughts that Jeremiah had about God (Jeremiah
20:11; 32:17)? Can you think of others?

_____

_____

_____

11. What did God tell Jeremiah was the only thing worth
boasting about (Jeremiah 9:23–24)?

_____

_____

_____

12. What part of this lesson made the greatest impact on
you?

_____

_____

_____

seven

A List of Demands,
Or a Life of Devotion?

One of the classic reasons people give for not praying is that they don't think God answers their prayers. We are taught that if we ask, we will receive. What if that doesn't seem to be the case? Should I expect God to answer *every* prayer? If He doesn't answer, is it because I don't have enough faith? Am I a spiritual failure?

We set ourselves up for failure when we view our spiritual life in terms of success and failure. If we view our spiritual life in these terms, we must have a way to measure results. This creates the need to quantify our quiet time in terms of frequency and duration or to keep track of the number of answers we receive for our requests.

I once read an article suggesting that we don't give ourselves credit for enough answers to prayer. The author suggested that we could boost our percentage of answers by noting that God answers in a variety of ways.

Give *ourselves* credit? Boost *our* percentage of answers? We are preoccupied with massaging our egos as we strive for spiritual "success." Too much of the focus of prayer tends to be on getting God to answer our demands. We bring our shopping list to God and then pride ourselves on being smart shoppers if God blesses us with an answer or two.

> If Elijah exemplifies effective prayer, then we should take a closer look at how prayer is modeled in his life.

But what does the Bible say about our "success" in prayer? James wrote to the early church, saying: "The effective prayer of a righteous man can accomplish much. Elijah was a man with a nature like ours, and he prayed earnestly that it would not rain, and it did not rain on the earth for three years and six months. Then he prayed again, and the sky poured rain and the earth produced its fruit" (5:16–18). So if Elijah exemplifies effective prayer, then we should take a closer look at how prayer is modeled in his life.

Elijah: "The Effective Prayer of a Righteous Man"

As Elijah walked the streets of Samaria, he was sickened to see the Asherah poles honoring the female deity and the massive house of Baal where thousands of people came to serve and worship this false god. Elijah longed for the days when his people worshipped the one true God. *Am I the only one,* he wondered, *who still worships and serves the Lord God of Israel?*

King Ahab used the royal treasury to fund these altars and shrines to false gods. He had done more to provoke the Lord than any other king. That's why the Lord had given Elijah this mission, though the thought of approaching the evil king made him shudder. As Elijah entered the courtyard of the house of Baal, he spotted the royal throne, sheltered from the intense heat by a fringed canopy. Elijah pushed his way through the throngs of people until he was as close as he could come to the royal throne. He raised his voice above the din of the crowd: "The Lord God of Israel lives! The Lord God of Israel lives!"

Ahab looked at him, a bit irritated by the intrusion of this religious fanatic.

Having the king's attention, Elijah continued, "There will not be dew or rain during these next years, except by my word." After making the proclamation according to the Word of the Lord, Elijah pushed his way back through the crowd. The stench of burnt offerings to Baal turned his stomach.

Ahab's irritation melted into amusement as he watched the strange man disappear into the crowd.

Elijah, repulsed by the foul stench of city life, camped by the brook Cherith. There the Lord commanded the ravens to bring Elijah food. Eventually, the lack of rain caused the brook to dry up, so the Lord told Elijah, "Go to Zarephath. I have commanded a widow there to provide for you."

Near the city gate, Elijah saw a widow gathering sticks. He asked her to bring him a little water to drink. As she turned to fetch the water, he called out, "And please bring me a piece of bread."

She dropped her sticks.

The woman returned to him with tears in her eyes and knelt down. "As the Lord lives, I have no bread. I was gathering sticks so that I might bake the last bit of flour and oil for my son and myself. After that, we will surely die."

Something about this man's eyes reassured the woman, even before he spoke. His voice was slow and gentle, but he spoke with authority. "Don't worry. Make me a little biscuit and bring it to me, then make one for yourself and your son. For the Lord promises you that your bowl of flour and jar of oil will not go empty until He again sends rain to this land."

The woman obeyed the word of Elijah, and, miraculously, the flour and oil jars did not go empty, though she used them daily.

During Elijah's stay with the widow, her son grew sick and died. In bitter pain, she lashed out at Elijah, "Have you come to put my son to death?"

Elijah took her son and laid him on his own bed. "My God, have you brought calamity to the widow with whom you commanded me to stay by causing her son to die? I pray, Lord, please let this child's life return to him." Elijah stretched himself upon the child three times, each time calling out to the Lord in the same way.

Then the Lord heard the voice of Elijah, and the child's life returned to him. When Elijah took the child downstairs, the woman could hardly believe her eyes. She embraced the child, and with tears streaking her face, she looked at Elijah: "Now I know that you are a man of God and that you speak the word of truth."

After three years of drought, the Lord spoke to Elijah: "Go confront Ahab and I will send rain on the earth."

As Elijah traveled to Samaria, he heard rumors that Ahab had searched every nation for three years looking for him, for the evil king sought to kill the prophet for bringing drought. However, Elijah's confidence in the Lord was unshaken by this news, so he went to meet Ahab.

"You blame me for this," said Elijah, "but you are to blame because you have forsaken the Lord and followed Baal. So gather all of Israel at Mount Carmel and bring all 450 of your Baal prophets and all 400 of the prophets of Asherah."

When all the people had gathered, Elijah called out: "How long will you waver between two opinions? If the Lord is God, follow Him; if Baal, follow him. We will prepare two oxen to sacrifice, and the prophets of Baal will call upon him, and I will call upon the Lord. The God who answers by fire, He is God."

So the prophets of Baal piled up wood and placed an ox upon it. Then they leaped about the altar, calling on the name of Baal from morning until noon.

Elijah mocked them: "Call out louder. Perhaps your god is asleep."

The prophets began to cut themselves, as was their custom, and they raved like lunatics until the evening, but there was no answer, and the people of Israel lost interest in their antics.

Finally, Elijah called the people to watch him. He took twelve stones to build an altar and made a trench around it. Then he arranged the wood and placed the ox on it. He had the people pour a dozen pitchers of water on the burnt offering until water not only soaked the wood but also filled the trench.

Elijah prayed, "Answer me, O Lord, that this people may know that you are God. Turn their hearts back to You."

Then fire fell from the Lord and consumed the burnt offering. Immediately the people fell to the ground, proclaiming, "The Lord is God. Surely, the Lord is God."

Then Elijah slew the prophets and proclaimed to Ahab that rain would come.

Elijah went up to the top of Mount Carmel and knelt in prayer, but he asked his servant to keep watch toward the sea.

"There is nothing," reported his servant.

"Look again," said Elijah.

Seven times he sent his servant back to look, but on the seventh time, he came back saying, "A small cloud is coming up from the sea."

As Ahab returned by chariot to Jezreel, the sky grew black with clouds. Finally, a heavy shower burst forth. Drenched with rain, Ahab raced through the doorway and told Jezebel, his wife, that Elijah had killed all of the prophets. She issued a death warrant, vowing to kill Elijah.

When Elijah heard it, he ran for his life, even leaving his servant behind. He traveled all night into the wilderness and sat down under a juniper tree. "I've had enough, Lord. Please take my life." Elijah fell asleep from exhaustion.

He awoke to find an angel touching him. The angel left him a bread cake baked on hot stones and a jar of water. Elijah ate and drank, then fell asleep again. The angel awoke him a second time, "Arise, eat, for you have a great journey ahead."

So Elijah ate and drank and traveled forty days to Horeb, the mountain of God.

Elijah stayed in a cave on Mount Horeb. "What are you doing here, Elijah?" asked the Lord.

"I have been very zealous for the Lord, but I am the last of your prophets, and they seek my life too."

The Lord said, "Go stand on the mountain." The Lord was passing by. A wind came up, so strong it was breaking rocks into pieces, but the Lord was not in the wind. Then an earthquake occurred, but the Lord was not in the earthquake. Then fire, but the Lord was not in the fire. After the fire, a sound of gentle blowing occurred. When Elijah heard it, he stood at the entrance of the cave.

"What are you doing here?" the Lord asked again.

"I have been very zealous for the Lord, but I am the last of your prophets, and they seek my life too."

The Lord said, "Anoint Hazael king over Aram and anoint Jehu king over Israel, then anoint Elisha as prophet in your place."

So Elijah did all that the Lord commanded and anointed Elisha to be the prophet of the Lord. When the time came for the Lord to take Elijah's life, Elijah asked Elisha, "Ask what I shall do for you before I am taken away."

Elisha said, "Please let a double portion of your spirit be upon me."

Elijah thought a moment and then responded carefully, "If you see me when I am taken, God will grant it; if not, it will not be done."

As they walked and talked, a chariot and horses of fire appeared between them. Then, Elisha watched as Elijah was taken up to heaven by a whirlwind.

Enough Faith

James pointed out that "Elijah was a man with a nature just like ours" (5:17). Elijah experienced spiritual and emotional highs and lows, just like the rest of us. He was not super-spiritual or supernatural; he was just an ordinary guy. Yet God used him in extraordinary ways because he prayed. So what made his prayers effective? And what if our prayers seem ineffective?

The disciples struggled with realizing that their prayers were not effective when they tried but could not cure a man's son (Matthew 17:14–20). They had done it before. Why didn't it work this time? As Jesus arrived on the scene, the man pleaded with Him to heal his son because the disciples could not. Jesus said, "You unbelieving and perverted generation . . . How long shall I put up with you?" (v. 17). Jesus rebuked the demon, and he came out of the boy.

Later, the disciples asked Jesus why they could not drive out the demon. "Because of the littleness of your faith," He said. Jesus explained, "If you have faith the size of a mustard seed, you will say to this mountain, 'Move from here to there,' and it will move" (v. 20).

Wait a minute. Jesus said they could not drive out the demon because of the "littleness" of their faith, but then He said that they needed faith only the size of a mustard seed, which is tiny. What does that mean? Exactly how much faith is enough?

When we see our prayers go unanswered, we shrug it off: "I guess I didn't have enough faith." We are baffled by the formula that God never seems to provide: How much faith is enough faith? Faith is not something we accumulate until we have "enough."

Perhaps we do not have faith to move mountains because

> Looking for a formula for "enough" faith? Our faith is in direct proportion to our need.

we misunderstand faith, just as the disciples did. The disciples thought they could heal the boy, but they could not. They had confidence: God had used them in this manner before. Still, they were unable because of the littleness of their faith.

Faith is admitting a simple truth: "I can't, but God can." The disciples thought they could accomplish a healing, so they had little faith. If they had realized that they couldn't do this on their own, it would have required greater faith: I can't chase away demons, but God can.

Looking for a formula for "enough" faith? Our faith is in direct proportion to our need. If we have to give a speech, we may ask God to help us through it. Often, in the back of our minds, we may be 90-percent confident that we can do it. Like the disciples, we know that we've done this before. Still, we are 10-percent nervous or uncertain. Essentially, we have 10-percent faith because we are asking God to make up only for what we lack in ourselves. However, someone with asthma may throw herself on God's feet, for without divine intervention, the stress of public speaking will certainly trigger an asthma attack. This person is placing 100-percent faith in God to get through this experience.

Hebrews 11:6 says, "And without faith it is impossible to please Him, for he who comes to God must believe that He is, and that He is a rewarder of those who seek Him." Now it makes sense: Without faith, we cannot please God because we are trusting only in ourselves. Faith places no confidence in the flesh (Philippians 3:3), but trusts God's unlimited power. Faith pleases God.

Elijah boldly believed God would withhold the rain. He could have looked foolish to proclaim such a thing if it did not occur. How many so-called prophets have announced that Jesus would return on a certain day, only to look foolish the day after He didn't return? For Elijah there was more at stake than looking foolish. According to Jewish law, when a prophet claimed to speak in the name of the Lord, and the thing prophesied did not come to pass, the prophet was sentenced to death.[1] So Elijah was betting his life on God.

---

1. See Deuteronomy 18:20–22. Similarly, even if the prophet spoke something that came true, but spoke in the name of other gods or spoke rebellion against God, he was to be put to death (Deuteronomy 13:1–5).

Although he was taking a risk, it was not risky, because he was assured that God would do it.

Effective prayer is an expression of bold faith. Hebrews 11:6 says that we must come to God in faith: God can! When our prayers are emboldened by this assurance, they are effective. Yet there remains a relational aspect: We come to God believing that "He is a rewarder of those who seek *Him.*" We must seek God, not spectacular results. God is not an on-call magician, but He will move mountains to clear the way for those who seek Him.

Effective Prayer

What makes prayer effective? Should we even be concerned about effectiveness? Doesn't this focus on quantifying results? These are valid questions, worthy of consideration.

James says, "The effective prayer of a righteous man can accomplish much" (5:16). A key element in this statement is that it is the prayer of a *righteous* man. We are not righteous within ourselves (Romans 3:10), but we share the righteousness of God by faith in Jesus Christ (Romans 3:21–22; Ephesians 4:24). The righteous live by faith (Romans 1:17), and faith is admitting, "I can't, but God can." The faith of a righteous person is the beginning of effective prayer.

Prayer is effective, or energized (the Greek word is *energeō*), by the Holy Spirit.[2] Romans 8:26–27 explains, "In the same way the Spirit also helps our weakness; for we do not know

2. In defining *energeō*, one scholar states: "In [James] 5:16 it seems to denote the inspired prayer or the prayer of a righteous man wrought by the operation or energy of the Holy Spirit (cf. Rom. 8:26, 27)." Spiros Zodhiates, ed., *Lexical Aids to the New Testament* in the *Hebrew-Greek Key Word Study Bible*, NASB edition, s.v. "energeō" (Chattanooga, Tenn.: AMG Publishers, 1990).

how to pray as we should, but the Spirit Himself intercedes for us with groanings too deep for words; and He who searches the hearts knows what the mind of the Spirit is, because He intercedes for the saints according to the will of God."

If the answer is not already clear, prayer is effective because of God, not us. We don't even know how to pray as we should. On our own, our prayers are ineffective. The Holy Spirit intercedes for us according to the will of God, making prayer effective. A prayer of faith by a righteous person could be compared to flipping a light switch, with the Holy Spirit providing the energy to produce a result. We don't need to quantify results because the results are in God's hands.

> A prayer of faith by a righteous person could be compared to flipping a light switch, with the Holy Spirit providing the energy to produce a result.

So, to paraphrase James 5:16: The prayer that is energized or empowered by God, offered up by someone who is in a right relationship with Him, can accomplish a great deal.

God's Will

It stands to reason that when we pray according to the will of God, our prayers will be effective and empowered by God.

After three years of drought, God told Elijah, "Go, show yourself to Ahab, and I will send rain on the face of the earth" (1 Kings 18:1). After Elijah confronted Ahab in the duel of the gods, Elijah knelt down and prayed for rain, the very thing God promised He would do.

Often we just need to add our amen to God's promises or God's revealed will. *Amen* means "make it so." It is a statement affirming God's trustworthiness. God promised it; surely it will come to pass. Amen! Make it so! Make it true in my life.

Do you want guaranteed prayer results? Whenever we pray from God's prayer list (which can be found in the Bible), we can be assured that He will grant our requests: "This is the confidence which we have before Him, that, if we ask anything according to His will, He hears us. And if we know that He hears us in whatever we ask, we know that we have the requests which we have asked from Him" (1 John 5:14–15). Praying from God's prayer list is a guarantee for effective, empowered prayer.

What exactly is on God's prayer list? In God's Word, there are a multitude of things that are God's revealed will for our lives. For example, the Bible says, "For this is the will of God, your sanctification; that is, that you abstain from sexual immorality (1 Thessalonians 4:3). Here's another list: "Rejoice always; pray without ceasing; in everything give thanks; for this is God's will for you in Christ Jesus" (1 Thessalonians 5:16–18). God's will is revealed throughout the Bible. We can ask that God make these things true in our lives, and we are guaranteed that God will make it so, for we already know these are things God wants to do in our lives.

Notice that these are relational prayers, not circumstantial prayers. That is, they focus on our relationship with God, the condition of our hearts, and the attitudes of our minds. For example, God's will is for our sanctification. We cannot make ourselves holy; our holiness comes from God. We can affirm to God that we want Him to make us holy—the very thing that He wants to do in us. We are guaranteed that such a prayer is effective and empowered.

God's will also includes meeting our basic needs. We've already discussed seeking God's provision as a needy suppliant, expressing our dependence on God to meet our needs. Jesus reminded His followers, "Your Father knows what you need before you ask Him," but He taught us to ask anyway: "Give us this day our daily bread" (Matthew 6:8, 11). Instead of worrying about what we will eat or drink or wear (v. 31), we are encouraged to take these concerns to God. Jesus concluded, "For your heavenly Father knows that you need all these things. But seek first His kingdom and His righteousness, and all these things will be added to you" (vv. 32–33). Although we are to seek God's provision, Jesus emphasized that we should seek God above all. There is a difference between loving the gift and loving the Giver. Remember, God is not a vending machine; He is our Lover who desires to meet our needs.

Look Again

Elijah knelt on Mount Carmel and prayed for what he already knew was God's will: that God would send rain. Seven times he sent his servant back, saying, "Look again." Seven times he prayed for rain.

If Elijah already knew that sending rain was God's will, wasn't one prayer sufficient? How do we know when to pray once and leave it in God's hands and when to persist in prayer?

Jesus warned against using "meaningless repetition" because "your Father knows what you need before you ask Him" (Matthew 6:7–8). In many cases we need to ask only once, for "how much more will your Father who is in heaven give what is good to those who ask Him!" (Matthew 7:11). We do not need to beg and plead to get God's blessing. Begging and pleading usually indicate that we are asking for something out of selfish motives: "You ask and do not receive, because you ask with wrong motives, so that you may spend it on your pleasures" (James 4:3). Think about how children act in a toy store after the parent tells them no. They think that begging, pleading, and even bargaining will get the results they desire. It's not that way with God. He knows what we need and is eager to give it to us when we admit our need rather than living in selfish independence, as if we didn't need God's help.

On the other hand, in His teaching about His second coming, Jesus told the disciples "that at all times they ought to pray and not to lose heart" (Luke 18:1). So how much should we pray about something?

The key is to pray until we have peace. If we are worried about something, we should continue to pray. Anything that disturbs our sense of peace is not of God, so we should continue to pray. For instance, we may lack peace if we are asking with selfish motives. Once we have surrendered our will to God on the matter, we sense the peace of being in harmony with God. Then our hearts are at peace, even if the results we seek are delayed. Sometimes we have peace knowing that our request is surrendered into God's hands, and we can rest and wait.

> We have peace knowing that our request is surrendered into God's hands, and we can rest and wait.

Prayer at Rest

When I was in seminary, our theology professor made a statement that rocked my world: "God is sovereign, and nothing we can do or say will change His mind."

My hand shot up. "If we cannot affect God's will or change His mind, then what's the point of praying?"

A collective gasp went through the room, which must have sucked all the oxygen out of the auditorium, because my face began to turn red, then purple.

"Is prayer about changing God's mind?" he asked.

This concept contradicted everything I had been taught to believe about prayer. Surely we petitioned God to make our case for why He should answer our prayers. Surely prayer made a difference. Surely prayer was effective. If God's mind were made up, then prayer seemed like a cruel joke. Only a sadistic egomaniac would allow others to ask, beg, and plead, just to watch them grovel.

I was so distraught that I sought out the dean, because I was prepared to quit praying altogether (and drop out of seminary) if prayer didn't matter.

She wisely pointed me to Psalm 131:2: "Surely I have composed and quieted my soul; like a weaned child rests against his mother, my soul is like a weaned child within me." An unweaned child comes to his mother's breast, making demands to be fed. A weaned child makes no demands but rests upon his mother's breast, accepting whatever she gives him at the moment.

So it is when we come to God in prayer. We can make demands, or we can rest in His presence and enjoy our intimate relationship. In a quiet time, we tend to present God with a list of demands, and our success or failure is measured by how well we get God to achieve our goals. Like a child in a toy store, we tend to think that if we ask enough times, God will change His mind and grant our request. However, prayer is not about changing God's mind; it's about changing our hearts.

> Prayer is not about changing God's mind; it's about changing our hearts.

When prayer becomes integrated into our whole life, there is no list of demands—just a life of total devotion. Instead of focusing on our success in getting God to achieve our goals, the focus turns to interaction with God for the sheer joy of it, like a weaned child. We gradually let go of our goals and accept whatever God has planned.

A LIST OF DEMANDS,
OR A LIFE OF DEVOTION?

1. What does James 5:16 say about effective prayer?

   _____

   _____

   _____

   Elijah: "The Effective Prayer of a Righteous Man"

2. James cites Elijah as an example of a person whose prayers were effective. List three things we learn about Elijah in James 5:17–18.

   1. _____

   2. _____

   3. _____

   Enough Faith

3. Faith is admitting, "I can't, but God can." In what areas do you need to make this proclamation of faith, admitting that you can't do it, but God can?

   _____

   _____

   _____

   _____

4. In Hebrews 11:6, we are reminded to come to God in faith (God can!), but are we to come seeking miraculous results? What is the relational aspect this verse points us toward?

_____

_____

_____

Effective Prayer

5. Prayer is effective because of God, not us. What does Romans 8:26–27 say about our effectiveness in prayer? What do these verses say about the Holy Spirit's effectiveness in prayer?

_____

_____

_____

God's Will

6. What do these verses say about prayer and God's will (Romans 8:26–27; 1 John 5:14–15)?

_____

_____

_____

7. If praying from God's prayer list is a guarantee for effective, empowered prayer, how can we know what is on God's prayer list?

_____

_____

_____

_____

8. Are we to seek answers to our circumstantial needs: What will we eat; what will we drink; what will we wear; how will we make the rent payment? What did Jesus say we should seek above all (Matthew 6:31–33)?

_____

_____

Look Again

9. What was God's will, as revealed to Elijah (1 Kings 18:1)? How many times did Elijah pray for God's will (1 Kings 18:41–45)?

_____

_____

10. What should we do when we know God's will and pray for it, but it does not immediately happen (Luke 18:1)?

_____

_____

Prayer at Rest

11. If we cannot affect God's will or change His mind, then what's the point of praying?

_____

_____

12. What is the lesson to be learned from Psalm 131:2?

_____

_____

_____

eight

A Devotion Explosion

*I*f the idea of growing more intimate with God still seems unattainable to you, consider this shocking reality: We are as close to God as we want to be. No exceptions, no excuses. Family background, past experience, or present circumstances cannot keep us from entering into an intimate relationship with God. We all tend to make excuses for not being more intimate with Him like, "I'd spend more time with God if . . . I had more time, a better education, a sympathetic family," or whatever. We are as close to God as we want to be, so we need to be aware of the excuses we may be making and take responsibility for our relationship with Him.

> As each intimate experience increases our love for God, our love, in turn, will increase our desire to share intimately with God. And so our love and intimacy with God grow without limits.

In light of this, are you ready for a devotion explosion? Do you want more of God than ever before?

As we begin to experience intimacy with God, our love for Him will expand to new capacities. Spending time with God in a variety of settings will

140

have a snowball effect: As each intimate experience increases our love for God, our love, in turn, will increase our desire to share intimately with God. And so our love and intimacy with God grow without limits.

Hezekiah had an intimate relationship with God, despite being the son of the most idolatrous king of Judah. Listen to what the Bible says about Hezekiah:

- He did right in the sight of the LORD (2 Kings 18:3).
- He removed the high places (2 Kings 18:4).
- He trusted in the LORD (2 Kings 18:5).
- After him there was none like him (2 Kings 18:5).
- He clung to the LORD (2 Kings 18:6).
- He did not depart from following Him (2 Kings 18:6).
- He kept His commandments (2 Kings 18:6).
- The LORD was with him (2 Kings 18:7).
- Wherever he went he prospered (2 Kings 18:7).
- He rebelled against the king of Assyria (2 Kings 18:7).
- He defeated the Philistines (2 Kings 18:8).

Hezekiah sounds like a superhero of faith, but he was actually an ordinary guy who found himself in extraordinary circumstances and clung to God in the midst of them.

Hezekiah: "He Clung to the LORD"

Hezekiah had hoped it wouldn't come to this, but deep down he knew this moment was inevitable. He had ruled as king of Judah for fourteen years. During that time he had cleaned up the royal mess his father, the wicked King Ahaz, had left to him. Unlike his father, Hezekiah followed the Lord earnestly. He removed all of the places of idol worship and destroyed all of the idols, including the most sacred one in Israel: the bronze serpent that Moses had made. What God intended as a symbol of salvation, Israel had made into an object of worship, burning incense to it from one generation to the next. Not only had he challenged the religious establishment, he also challenged the king of Assyria. Hezekiah's father had sold out to the king of Assyria by ransacking the house of God for any valuables to pay tribute, bribing the king of Assyria to become his ally and protector. During the fourth year of Hezekiah's reign, the king of Assyria had captured Samaria and taken the Israelites captive. Hezekiah knew that if this invasion could happen to his neighbors in Israel, it was only a matter of time until it happened to Judah. That was ten years ago. Now, as Hezekiah watched the vast armies of Assyria capture city after city in Judah, he was having second thoughts about his decision to stand up to this bully nation.

"Quickly," beckoned Hezekiah, "send this message to the king of Assyria: 'I was wrong to stop paying tribute. Withdraw from the cities of Judah, and I will pay the price, no matter what.'"

As he waited for a reply, Hezekiah found himself second-guessing his second guesses. What could be done to save his crumbling nation? The messenger returned with the sum demanded by Assyria. Though it pained him to do so, Hezekiah stripped the silver and gold from the house of God and gave it to the king of Assyria.

After all that, what thanks did he get? Instead of sending an envoy of goodwill ambassadors, the king of Assyria sent his vast army to camp on the doorstep of Jerusalem. Terror, anger, frustration, and dismay filled Hezekiah's heart with turmoil as he watched and waited. He knew this time would come, and now it was here.

Each day, the officials of the Assyrian army would harass the inhabitants of Jerusalem, calling out to them over the city wall, declaring that Hezekiah's God could not save them from the Assyrian army. The Assyrians pleaded with the people of Jerusalem to surrender: "Do not let Hezekiah mislead you, saying, 'The Lord will deliver us.' The gods of the other lands, including Israel, were not able to save them from the mighty hand of Assyria. Or do you not know that the Lord sent us to destroy your land, just as we destroyed Israel?"

Hezekiah tore his royal clothes off and put on sackcloth to convey his deep sorrow and anguish. He entered the house of the Lord and felt the deep pain of seeing how he had stripped the Lord's house only to have it come down to this. He sent for the prophet Isaiah, who encouraged Hezekiah with a word from the Lord: "The servants of the king of Assyria have blasphemed Me, so do not be afraid. I will cause him to return to his own land."

Sure enough, the army officials heard that the Assyrian king was fighting against a different city, so they prepared to leave to support him. As they were leaving, they sent a letter to Hezekiah: "Do not let your God deceive you by saying, 'Jerusalem will not fall into the hands of Assyria.' We'll be back to destroy you, just as we destroyed the other nations, whose gods were unable to save them."

Hezekiah took the letter up to the house of the Lord and spread it out before the Lord, praying, "Lord, You alone are God of all the kingdoms of the earth. Listen to the words of this letter. It is true that Assyria has destroyed every other nation they have set their sights on and have destroyed their gods, but they were merely wood and stone, that Assyria should destroy them. So I pray that You would deliver us from the hand of Assyria so that all of the kingdoms of the earth would know that You alone are God."

The Lord responded through Isaiah the prophet, saying, "Because you prayed to Me about Assyria, I have heard your prayer. The king of Assyria will not come to this city, for I will defend this city for My own sake."

At first light the next morning, the watchmen on the walls initially thought the enemy army was asleep, but, as the light increased, they realized that the entire Assyrian army had been slain. During the night, the angel of the Lord went through the camp and struck 185,000 Assyrians—the entire army—dead.

Hezekiah had been nursing a boil, but as it grew worse, he became bedridden. Isaiah came to his bedside. "I have a word from the Lord," he said to his old friend. Hezekiah's face brightened. Isaiah grasped his friend's hand and spoke softly: "The Lord says, 'Put your house in order, for you will die.'"

Hezekiah rolled over to face the wall and wept bitterly. He prayed, "Lord, I beg You, remember how I have walked before you and served you with my whole heart."

Before Isaiah had left the king's courtyard, the Lord prompted him to go back to Hezekiah. He entered to find Hezekiah still weeping. "Hezekiah, the Lord says 'I have heard your prayer and seen your tears. I will heal you and add fifteen years to your life. Moreover, I will deliver you from the hand of Assyria.'"

"Prove it," Hezekiah managed to choke out between sobs.

Isaiah looked kindly upon his suffering friend, "The Lord will give you a sign. Do you want the shadow to move forward ten steps or back ten steps?"

Hezekiah looked at the stairs and answered, "The shadow naturally moves forward on the steps, so let the shadow turn back so I will know it is from God."

Isaiah prayed to the Lord, and God moved the shadow on the stairway back ten steps, which it had already gone down.

When the king of Babylon heard that Hezekiah had been sick, he sent letters and a present to Hezekiah. By now, however, Hezekiah had been healed, so he showed the ambassadors around the royal house, including all of the treasure in the royal treasuries. As the ambassadors were leaving, Isaiah pulled Hezekiah aside: "Who are those men and what have they seen?"

Hezekiah proudly replied, "They came to pay their respects from Babylon, so I showed them my great wealth."

Isaiah shook his head in dismay. "The Lord says that all your treasures will one day be carried off to Babylon, and your sons will serve the king of Babylon."

"Well," Hezekiah responded thoughtfully, "at least there will be peace during the rest of my lifetime."

Free to Cling

Crisis tends to drive people to or away from God. How about you? Is your first instinct to run to God for safety and comfort or to back away wondering if you can trust a God who allows such a thing? If the latter describes you, there is hope (I used to be that person). You can learn to trust God.

There is a remarkable product on the market that removes static cling from your clothes, but those little dryer sheets possess their own remarkable form of "smart" cling. That is, they cling to the inside of your pants leg until the most inopportune moment. They are smart enough to know when to let go to provide the optimum embarrassment. Your clothes may be cling-free, as advertised, but not the little white phantom of pants.

In the records of the kings of Judah, Hezekiah is memorialized this way: "He clung to the LORD" (2 Kings 18:6). In times of distress, we must cling to God as if our lives depended on it. When times are darkest, when God might feel far away, hang on to God and refuse to let go. We can pursue God with all the tenacity of a dryer sheet.

Part of that tenacity will come as we engage God consistently throughout all aspects of our lives. As we gain firsthand experience that God is trustworthy, we will find ourselves free to cling: free from doubts and free to embrace God. As we gain confidence from clinging to Him, our faith grows.

Character Counts

When faced with a personal health crisis, Hezekiah clung to God. The Lord told him the sickness, a boil, would be fatal. Hezekiah prayed and wept before the Lord, appealing to God to reverse His decision and heal him. As Hezekiah prayed for his recovery, he reminded the Lord of "how I have walked before You in truth and with a whole heart and have done what is good in Your sight" (2 Kings 20:3).

Apparently, appealing to his own faithfulness was effective, for God acknowledged that He heard Hezekiah's prayer

(2 Kings 20:5). We must be careful here, for we cannot fall into a works mentality that weighs the good and bad in our life. We are justified by faith—and faith alone. Hezekiah was not simply appealing to all of the good things he had done; he was appealing to a faithful heart, characterized by whole-hearted obedience.

Hezekiah was not the only one to cry out to the Lord to save him from death. Christ did the same: "In the days of His flesh, He offered up both prayers and supplications with loud crying and tears to the One able to save Him from death, and *He was heard because of His piety*" (Hebrews 5:7, emphasis added). Hezekiah appealed to his own faithfulness, and Christ was heard because of His piety.

Character counts. It is good to remind ourselves of this truth: "Behold, the LORD's hand is not so short that it cannot save; nor is His ear so dull that it cannot hear. But your iniquities have made a separation between you and your God, and your sins have hidden His face from you so that He does not hear" (Isaiah 59:1–2). God cannot hear our prayers when we come to Him with dirty hands—unless, of course, we bring our dirty hands so He can wash them (1 John 1:9).

> Nothing reveals the contents of our hearts more than the way we pray. Our prayers reveal what we believe about God, our circumstances, and ourselves.

Nothing reveals the contents of our hearts more than the way we pray. Our prayers reveal what we believe about God, our circumstances, and ourselves. They disclose whether our motives are selfish or if we truly desire to glorify God, and they uncover the sinful thoughts and attitudes lurking beneath the surface of our lives. We can hide our true thoughts from everyone but God:

"You understand my thought from afar . . . Even before there is a word on my tongue, Behold, O LORD, You know it all" (Psalm 139:2–4).

That Reminds Me

Our thoughts are like billiard balls: as they collide with each other, they take radically new directions. People often complain that they experience wandering thoughts when they pray. They struggle to stay focused with all the other thoughts banging around in their heads. Some people suggest writing down their stray thoughts so they can stay on track. However, it may be a good idea to follow those thoughts, wherever they may lead!

First, the notion of staying on track implies that you know the track you should stay on—you set the agenda—but maybe God is bringing things to mind that are on His agenda for discussion.

Second, whatever is on our minds is something worth talking to God about. Perhaps you keep thinking about your dentist appointment because you need to surrender your anxiety to God.

Third, God already knows our thoughts, so we don't need to make a real distinction between our thoughts and prayers. It's not like we need to push aside our thoughts to focus on formal prayer, because every thought has been "read" by the Holy Spirit within us. The more we maintain a spirit of prayer in the midst of our thoughts throughout the day, the closer we come to praying without ceasing (1 Thessalonians 5:17).

I was recently on an eight-mile hike with a friend. The temperature was in the nineties, and by the second half of the hike, we were beginning to suffer. I silently longed to take off my hot boots and dip my aching feet in a cool stream, but a summer drought had dried up all of the mountain streams.

Somewhere between miles six and seven, we encountered a small waterfall. Ice cold glacier water gently spilled over a few rocks and collected in a small pool. We shed our heavy boots and submerged our feet in the icy water gently flowing over the mossy rocks. We sat there laughing and praising God, thanking Him for creating that water for our enjoyment.

God knew my thoughts: I longed to put my hot feet in cold water. It may as well have been a prayer: God heard my desire and answered it. God lavished His love on me, and my pleasure in His gift gave God great joy—all because God knew my thoughts, even though I had not formally addressed them to Him.

The Big Picture

Hezekiah integrated God into his whole life. He prayed both personally and professionally. Whether he faced a personal health crisis or a besieging army that posed a national crisis, Hezekiah took every need to God.

When Hezekiah received a letter from his enemies, he "took the letter from the hand of the messengers and read it, and he went up to the house of the LORD and spread it out before the LORD. Hezekiah prayed" (2 Kings 19:14–15). That's a powerful image. We would do well to spread our problems out before the Lord and pray about them.

It's easy to get caught up in our little world, praying according to our selfish desires. It's not so easy to step back and look at the big picture of what God may be doing in a larger scheme than our narrow-minded self-interests.

When Assyria had surrounded Jerusalem, Hezekiah could have asked God to save the people for their sake, but instead, Hezekiah asked God to do so for His sake. He prayed "deliver us from his hand that all the kingdoms of the earth may know that You alone, O LORD, are God" (2 Kings 19:19).

When we consider God's perspective, we catch a glimpse of God's plan and purpose. In the midst of our crisis, our desperate circumstances, God is already at work. It's up to us to recognize His work and align ourselves with it.

Holy Cows and Sacred Snakes

Hezekiah was the son of Ahaz, the worst king in the history of Judah. Yet family background didn't hinder Hezekiah's walk with God. Instead, it sharpened his focus on the things that needed to change once he was in a position to make changes.

Don't excuse yourself from wholehearted devotion to God just because of your family circumstances, either past or present. It's easy to think: *Well, I wish I knew the Bible better or had a better relationship with God, but I didn't have the advantage of being raised in a Christian home.* Or, *Because my spouse doesn't serve God, I'll never be able to have the relationship with God that I want.* Those are excuses. As I mentioned at the beginning of the chapter, you are as close to God as you want to be. You can't change the past (and God placed you in that family for a reason), but you can make the most of the present, even if your spouse doesn't join you in service to God.

After watching the religious degradation of his father's reign, Hezekiah knew the dangerous power of religious symbols. In the process of cleaning house, Hezekiah removed all of the religious symbols—the holy cows—used in the worship of false gods, including the most appalling of all: the bronze serpent that Moses had made (2 Kings 18:4). What was this bronze serpent?

Moses led the Israelites through the desert, but they were a bunch of nagging complainers, so God sent fiery serpents among them (Numbers 21:6-9), and people who were bitten by these poisonous snakes died. Moses interceded for the people, so God, in His mercy, instructed Moses to make a bronze serpent and raise it up on a pole. If anyone was bitten, they could look at the bronze serpent and live. It required an act of faith.

Unfortunately, that which God intended as a temporary symbol of His saving mercy became a permanent object of worship among the Israelites for generations to come. Until Hezekiah destroyed the bronze serpent, "the sons of Israel burned incense to it; and it was called Nehushtan" (2 Kings 18:4). Exceeding its intended purpose, this symbol had taken on a life of its own.[1]

1. The gospel of John compares the bronze serpent to the cross of Christ. For just as Israel looked to the serpent with faith that God would save them, we now look to Christ with faith that God will save us: "As Moses lifted up the serpent in the wilderness, even so must the Son of Man be lifted up; so that whoever believes will in Him have eternal life. For God so loved the world, that He gave His only begotten Son, that whoever believes in Him shall not perish, but have eternal life" (John 3:14–16). Perhaps the cross of Christ can be compared to a modern bronze serpent in that we have taken the symbol of the cross and turned it into jewelry, home décor, and bumper stickers. I fear that, for some, the cross has become nothing more than a good luck charm—a modern idol. We must be careful to remember that the cross does not save us; it merely represents the loving mercy of God who saves us.

There is an important lesson here. When religious symbols, liturgies, prayers, or forms of devotion become the object of our attention, they must be discarded in order to return our affection to the God those symbols and forms were intended to exalt.

To put it another way, if maintaining a stellar quiet time is the goal, and not devotion to God, then it is time to quit your quiet time. A quiet time is a form or structure intended to help us focus the devotion of our heart toward God. However, the form itself has no significance.

It might be useful to think of a structured quiet time as training wheels. Eventually—hopefully sooner rather than later—the training wheels become unnecessary and may even get in the way. It is intended to be so. When the training wheels outlive their usefulness, they must be discarded. More importantly, if the training wheels become sacred, they must be destroyed.

Fat and Happy

Perhaps you picked up this book because you knew that your quiet time wasn't working, no matter what you tried. You long for intimacy with God, but for some reason it has eluded you. Maybe you perceived God as far away rather than living within you. Maybe God didn't seem like a real person with Whom you could have a real relationship. Maybe you were afraid to get close to God because of sin in your life, hurts from the past, or fearful expectations of what God might ask of you if you fully surrendered to Him.

The reassuring thing is that God knows everything about us, and He loves us just the way we are (sin and all), but He loves us so much that He doesn't want to leave us mired in the pain, sin, and fear that keep us from an intimate relationship with Him. He longs to give Himself wholly to each of us. We can be completely satisfied in Him.

No one makes Swiss steak like my mom. Whenever my birthday or a special occasion comes around, she rolls up her sleeves and spends all afternoon preparing my favorite meal. With flour flying, grease spattering, tomato sauce oozing out from under the lid of her electric skillet, and a sink full of messy dishes, it truly is a labor of love. The aroma of the sautéed onions and warm tomato sauce makes my mouth water long before the meal is served. The anticipation stimulates my appetite. When we all sit down for dinner, I pile my plate with rice and meat, then slather it with tomato sauce—and usually go back for seconds. I enjoy this meal a little too much and push myself away from the table with that fat and happy feeling.

God wants each of us to have that fat and happy feeling in Him. Paul prayed that believers would "know the love of Christ which surpasses knowledge, that you may be *filled up to all the fullness of God* (Ephesians 3:19, emphasis added). As big as God is, you can be filled up with God! Fat and happy!

Joanna Weaver writes, "We were created for the fullness of God, not an ounce or liter less. But are we ready for that? After all, being filled to the measure with all the fullness of God will most likely require our being stretched. At the very least, it is sure to disturb our comfort." The same way our stomach stretches as we eat too much food—until we are uncomfortably full—God wants to stretch our lives to hold all of Him. I've wondered how much I can eat before my stomach explodes, but maybe I should be wondering how much of God I can hold before I explode. Weaver challenges us to ask ourselves, "Are we willing to let God explode our comfort zone and expand our capacity for him? Or do we want a God we can manage?"[2]

It's comfortable to have a God we can manage. With God as our co-pilot, we control our flight plan through life and bark orders when we need help. It's convenient to take God out of the box for half an hour, then put Him away so He doesn't make too much of a mess of our lives. But is that a very satisfying way to live? Wouldn't you rather develop the intimacy that you long for? Do you want just a little bit of God, or do you want to be filled up to all the fullness of God? Are you ready for a devotion explosion?

The Big Bang

I'm hoping that you will have a big-bang experience—a devotion explosion! If you have been shackled with rules and fettered by formulas that you learned from other believers, may the explosion free you from all expectations—yours or someone else's. If you have been burdened by the duty of daily devotions, may the explosion free you from the guilt of perpetual failure despite your best efforts. In short, I hope that you have found the ideas in this book liberating, because intimacy with God develops as we share every experience with Him, rather than when we limit our communication to a daily appointment.

2. Joanna Weaver, *Having a Mary Heart in a Martha World: Finding Intimacy with God in the Busyness of Life* (Colorado Springs, Colo.: WaterBrook Press, 2002), 104.

I quit my quiet time because nurturing any relationship, especially with the One who loved me enough to die for me, should not be perceived as a duty that breeds guilt. Intimacy with God is not a matter of being more disciplined or finding the right formula; it's a matter of cultivating a desire to spend every moment with One who is more desirable than any substitute.

> When a devotion explosion occurs in our lives, we find that we can't spend enough time with God.

When a devotion explosion occurs in our lives, we find that we can't spend longer and longer periods of time in God's Word. We look forward to every opportunity to converse with God. "Devotions," in the mechanical sense, become a thing of the past. "Devotions" are quickly replaced by true devotion to God.

A DEVOTION EXPLOSION

1. "I'd spend more time with God if . . ."
   "I'd have a better relationship with God if . . ."
   What excuses do you use to justify your lack of intimacy with God?

   _____

   _____

   _____

   Hezekiah: "He Clung to the Lord"

2. What does the Bible say about Hezekiah (2 Kings 18:3–8)?

   _____

   _____

   _____

   Free to Cling

3. Hezekiah clung to the Lord (2 Kings 18:6). What keeps you from clinging to God?

   _____

   _____

   _____

4. Crisis tends to drive people to or away from God. Which describes you? Think of an example of how you handled a crisis with or without God. Would you

handle that situation differently now, and if so, how would you do things differently?

_____

_____

_____

Character Counts

5. Why does character count when we pray (Hebrews 5:7; Isaiah 59:1–2)? What might be separating you from God, hindering your prayers?

_____

_____

_____

6. Take time to ask for God's forgiveness. Write out 1 John 1:9. Why is it important to bring our dirty hands and hearts to God so He can wash them?

_____

_____

_____

That Reminds Me

7. People often complain of wandering thoughts when they pray. What do you do when you feel distracted while talking to God? Why might you want to follow those wandering thoughts wherever they lead?

_____

_____

_____

The Big Picture

8. When we consider situations from God's perspective, how might it change the way we pray?

_____

_____

_____

Holy Cows and Sacred Snakes

9. Hezekiah removed all of the religious symbols—the holy cows—used in the worship of false gods, including the most appalling of all: the bronze serpent that Moses had made. What was the original intent of this bronze serpent, and how was it now being misused (Numbers 21:6–9; 2 Kings 18:4)?

_____

_____

_____

_____

10. A quiet time is a form or structure intended to help us focus our heart toward God. Do you feel that the form helps or hinders your devotion toward God? In what way? Is your focus on the form or on God?

_____

_____

_____

Fat and Happy

11. Do you want just a little bit of God, or do you want to be filled up to all the fullness of God? What fears

do you have about fully surrendering your life to God?

_____

_____

_____

The Big Bang

12. What steps can you take to experience a devotion explosion in your life?

_____

_____

_____

Take time to write out a prayer expressing your desire to develop greater intimacy with God. Use a separate sheet if desired.

_____

_____

_____

_____

_____

_____

_____

_____

_____

_____

_____

_____

_____

Note to the Reader

The publisher invites you to share your response to the message of this book by writing Discovery House Publishers, Box 3566, Grand Rapids, MI 49501, USA. For information about other Discovery House books, music, or videos, contact us at the same address or call 1-800-653-8333. Find us on the Internet at http://www.dhp.org/ or send e-mail to books@ dhp.org.